Excuse My French!

Rachel Best (a rosbif) and Jean-Christophe Van Waes (a frog) met on an Italian ski slope and fell in love. Then came the miscomprehensions, mistranslations and frequent sheer bewilderment as they struggled to make themselves understood. **Excuse My French!** is the result of their hard-won experience and an essential primer on how to communicate successfully, how not to inadvertently insult your partner and how to maintain harmonious relations.

Excuse My French!

Fluent Français Without the Faux Pas

RACHEL BEST
AND
JEAN-CHRISTOPHE VAN WAES

Kyle Books

First published in Great Britain in 2013 by
Kyle Books
192–198 Vauxhall Bridge Road
London, SW1V 1DX
general.enquiries@kylebooks.com
www.kylebooks.com

ISBN: 978-0-85783-169-9

10 9 8 7 6 5 4

Editor: Vicki Murrell
Designer: Peter Ward
Copy-editor: Caroline Taggart
Production: Gemma John, Lisa Pinnell and Nic Jones

A Cataloguing In Publication record for this title is available
from the British Library

Printed and bound by CPI Group (UK) Ltd, Croydon, CR0 4YY

CONTENTS

How it all began

The French and the English have been 'frenemies' (sometimes friends, sometimes enemies) ever since an intrepid soul managed to cross the Channel, or La Manche. Can't live with them, can't live without them, so what better response than to insult them in metaphors and slang?

The Limeys call them 'the Frogs'. En revanche, the Gaulois call the island dwellers 'Les Rosbifs'.

A French kiss to the French is 'une pelle' (*a shovel*)

A French letter is known as 'une capote anglaise'.

If you didn't use one, you might catch the 'French disease' ('la chtouille'), also known as syphilis.

Yikes.

Or you could:

Take French leave
Filer à l'anglaise *(To make off English style)*

....

This expression, which means to sneak away without permission, is a good barometer of the state of Anglo-French relations. The English version dates back to the 18th century and arose from the French custom of leaving a social gathering without explicitly informing the host/hostess of their imminent departure. Perfectly acceptable in French society, bad form in polite English company. It seems the French were not just skulking off from English get-togethers, since the Germans, Portuguese and Spanish also invoke the French in expressions with similar meanings. For their part, the French associated the English with a whole range of socially unacceptable behaviour. 'Anglaiser' used to mean to steal, un 'Anglais' in the Middle Ages was a loan never to be repaid since the debtor absconded first. Indeed, by the 19th century, 'pisser à l'anglaise' was to be found in the books of Zola, where it referred to someone sneaking off to relieve themselves without asking for authorisation. Which is worst?

This sets the scene for *Excuse my French!*, an expression traditionally used when you swear or blaspheme in English, and then try to pretend you haven't by implying what you said was actually in another language: French!

For us – Rachel (English) and Jean-Christophe (French) – the idea for this book arose out of the difficulties and culture clash of life in a bilingual couple. After endless miscomprehensions, mistranslations and often sheer bewilderment at what the Rosbif was trying to say to the Gaul, we decided to start a collection of expressions. Though neither a grammar study nor a serious dictionary, the book should help anyone striving to speak either foreign language like a local, and hopefully give you a laugh along the way. It aims to be a light-hearted look at cultural and linguistic differences between the French and English nations, which belie the two countries' geographical proximity and the Entente Cordiale.

Though the book is by no means exhaustive, we hoped to create an amusing selection of phrases to cover the most important aspects of daily life – work, money, sex etc. Our choice of expressions is subjective, and we are sure you could provide your own alternative idioms. We look forward to reading them. We have tried to give some background on a selection of the phrases we found interesting. These are not authoritative definitions, rather suggestions as to the origins of the expressions derived from a number of different sources. In the interests of European harmony, we have also made occasional reference to how our European neighbours might express certain phrases differently to the French or English.

Dip in, dip out of the book. Try the quiz at the start of each chapter to test your knowledge in advance. Watch out for expressions marked with (!), as these are more appropriate for a raucous night out in Pigalle or Soho than for afternoon tea with the Queen. And to save you reaching constantly for the dictionary, there is a glossary of less familiar French words at the back.

Above all, we hope you enjoy reading the book as much as we did writing it, despite all the spitting and cursing. *\$@%! Excuse my French!

Rachel and Jean-Christophe

PEOPLE ARE STRANGE

LES GENS SONT BIZARRES

THERE'S NOWT SO QUEER AS FOLK, as we say in Yorkshire. In speech and deed people can be annoying in any language. Bad habits, laziness, even insanity are all traits we don't admire in our fellow man. However, it isn't all bad and, fortunately for the future of the human race, there are many human beings with redeeming features. You may not like all of them, but at least you may find the words to describe them in this chapter.

QUIZ

Try to match up the following phrases.
Redemption is at the end of the chapter . . .

1. Un second couteau
2. Ne pas avoir inventé le fil à couper le beurre
3. Souple comme un verre de lampe
4. Etre fainéant comme une couleuvre
5. Une histoire à dormir debout
6. Sage comme une image
7. Avoir froid aux yeux
8. Tout sucre, tout miel

a) As stiff as a board
b) A cock-and-bull story
c) Small fry
d) To be bone idle
e) To be not the sharpest knife in the drawer
f) To be a scaredy cat
g) All sweetness and light
h) As good as gold

Full of it!

JE ME LA RACONTE

Able to talk the hind leg off a donkey
Bavard comme une pie

A chatterbox
Un moulin à paroles

These expressions mean almost the same thing: the person in question talks too much! Possibly the second English one is stronger than the first, but both date from late 18th/early 19th century. We don't know exactly how it came to be the poor donkey whose leg was to be withered away by incessant talking, but it started off being a horse and then a dog before the phrase settled into its current form. The first French expression chosen here also exists in English, though it is not commonly used. To be a magpie is to be extremely loquacious (and annoying with it, as magpies are when they are squawking at full volume). The mill ('moulin') mentioned in the second French phrase refers to something which churns out a product incessantly without reference to the quality or even the quantity of what is being produced. The idiom dates back to at least the 18th century, which means that people have been talking too much for a very long time on both sides of the Channel...

She had to stick her oar in
Elle n'a pas pu s'empêcher de mettre son grain de sel

She (but it doesn't have to be a woman) is a meddler. Someone who just can't resist becoming involved and often without anyone asking her to. The English version is one of many nautical idioms in the Rosbif language and probably dates from the 17th century. The imagery is clear: a boat is moving through the water quite efficiently under paddle-power, until one bright spark decides she will 'help' it along by rowing alongside. She has stuck her oar in, and most probably messed up the rhythm of the boat. The French version has its roots in Roman times, being based on Pliny's *cum grano salis* (with a pinch of salt). Historically, this had a positive sense of adding or contributing to a discussion, but the French expression, which dates from the 20th century, uses the concept ironically. One really didn't need that particular extra grain of salt, merci beaucoup. Interestingly, the English phrase 'to take it with a pinch of salt', or to be sceptical/doubtful of something, has the same etymological root. Note that the Germans refer to someone adding their mustard to something to express the same idea.

To always shout at the top of one's voice
Crier comme un sourd *(To shout like a deaf person)*

To be a right nosy parker
Etre une vraie fouine *(To be a real stone marten)*

To never say a word
Etre muet comme une carpe *(To be as mute as a carp)*

To be all mouth and no trousers
Avoir une grande gueule et de petits bras
(To have a big gob and small arms)

To tell a cock-and-bull story Raconter une histoire à dormir debout
(To tell a story to sleep standing up)

To be a nasty piece of work
Etre mauvais comme la gale *(To be as bad as scabies)*

Boys will be boys Il faut que jeunesse se passe *(Youth needs to pass)*

To think you're God's gift…
Se croire sorti de la cuisse de Jupiter

…to women is the usual conclusion of the English version, but both expressions can refer to someone who overestimates their intelligence or capabilities, not just their attractiveness to the opposite sex. The English version is clear: someone thinks they are so perfect that they are God's personal gift to mankind. Such modesty. The French version also invokes a god, though this time it is the mythical Jupiter (or Zeus to the Greeks). Roman mythology tells how the mortal Semele, impregnated by the god, almost perished in the brilliance of Jupiter's full apparition to her and risked losing the unborn baby Bacchus (or Dionysus). Jupiter took the embryo and implanted it in his leg, whereupon, after a further three months' gestation, a perfect baby demi-god was born.

What's wrong with you?
C'EST QUOI TON PROBLÈME ?

Like a bull in a china shop
Comme un éléphant dans un magasin de porcelaine

In either language this could be an expensive occupation, since the expressions describe someone who is very clumsy or maladroit. It is difficult to decide which animal might do more damage. The elephant is bigger, so could destroy more fragile china plates. On the other hand, the bull might be smaller, but has a reputation for having a mean temper, and you can imagine it bucking and kicking in an attempt to make its escape. The English expression dates from the early 19th century, but the date of the French one is unknown. In their equivalent expressions, both the Germans and the Spanish choose an elephant over a bull, whereas the Italians, being more delicate of touch, cite mice in the bell-tower.

Like a fish out of water
Pas dans son élément

This expression describes someone ill at ease in their environment. The unfortunate English fish on dry land, flapping about out of water, has been on record since the 19th century, though it is likely it was known in common parlance before then. Interestingly, a positive form of the expression 'like a fish in water' exists in both languages and the French version 'Il est comme un poisson dans l'eau' can be traced as far back as the 13th century. Equally, references to being in your element (or not) also exist in both French and English, and have done since at least the 16th century. These elements originally referred to the four primary humours (air, fire, earth and water) which were believed to dictate the disposition and character of humans. Keeping these in balance was thus paramount to a harmonious and happy life.

To be fingers and thumbs
Avoir deux mains gauches *(To have two left hands)*

To have a poker up your arse (!)
Avoir un balai dans le cul *(To have a broom up your arse)*

To have a stick up your bum
Etre vraiment constipé *(To be really constipated)*

The black sheep of the family Le vilain petit canard de la famille
(The bad little duck of the family)

As stiff as a board Souple comme un verre de lampe
(As flexible as a glass chimney lamp)

She won't budge an inch Elle ne cèdera pas d'un pouce

As stubborn as a mule Têtu comme une mule

He's going to blow a fuse Il va piquer une crise *(He's going to sting a fit)*

Small fry Un second couteau *(A second knife)*

Like a cat on a hot tin roof
Nerveux comme une puce *(Nervous as a flea)*

A sitting duck Une cible facile *(An easy target)*

To be a scaredy cat Avoir froid aux yeux *(To have cold eyes)*

To go off at a tangent
Passer du coq à l'âne
....

To be prone to change the subject without warning or to introduce a non sequitur. The English version derives originally from mathematics, in which a tangential line is one that runs alongside another, touching but not intersecting with it. In the same way, when someone goes off at a tangent, the new subject might be related, but doesn't necessarily follow from the original line of argument. The French version has a more enigmatic etymology. The expression itself is very old, dating from the 14th century in a similar form, but appears to have been corrupted over the years. The modern translation is 'To pass (or jump if 'sauter' is used) from the cockerel to the donkey'. Nonsensical, as indeed many tangential conversations are. However it seems that 'l'âne' (donkey) was originally 'la cane' (female duck) and the verb used was 'saillir' (to jut out), which in ancient times had a more salacious meaning of 'to mount'. Hence we have a suspected farmyard sexual infraction with a cockerel attempting to mate with a female duck. Perhaps it is time to change the subject again? The Walloons talk from 13 to 14 and the Italians jump from the post to the branch, while the Dutch jump from the heel to the branch to express the same non sequitur.

Not quite what they seem
LES APPARENCES SONT TROMPEUSES

A goody two-shoes
Une sainte-nitouche
....

The French, which means someone who behaves impeccably, but is rather smug about it, can be found in in the 16th-century writings of Rabelais. There is no actual saint called 'nitouche', and the word was originally a play on 'n'y toucher' or someone who isn't to be touched, and certainly not by what men keep tucked away in their trousers. The current phrase 'faire la sainte-nitouche' communicates this sense of hypocrisy, as it is used for someone who claims not to be interested, for whom butter wouldn't melt in their mouth, but who in reality is the opposite. The English version dates from the mid-18th century and originates in the writing of Oliver Goldsmith. *The History of Little Goody Two-Shoes*, written in 1765, is a nursery tale with a moral. Goody, a poor little girl, had only one shoe, but when someone gave her a pair, she ran around proudly telling all and sundry that she had 'two shoes'.

Butter wouldn't melt in her mouth
On lui donnerait le bon Dieu sans confession

This is something one could possibly say about Goody Two-Shoes, since it means that a person appears more demure or innocent than could possibly be the case. The English version was first recorded in 1530 in a work by John Palsgrave called *L'esclarcissement de la langue françoyse*. Interestingly, the idiom does not seem to exist in the French language of today. Possibly it derives from the fact that the person concerned is so saintly, perhaps as holy as a marble statue of a religious figure, that he or she is cool to the touch and thus unable to melt butter by body heat alone. The French expression has a more overt religious tone. It refers to the ceremony of the Catholic Church whereby, after confessing one's sins to the priest, one is deemed worthy to commune with and finally meet with God. In our expression the person is so innocent and pure that they can sidestep the confessional and go straight to God Himself.

He can't see the wood for the trees
C'est l'arbre qui cache la forêt

This means to get so lost in the detail that you can no longer see the bigger picture. The English version dates at least from the 16th century as Heywood's *Dialogue of Proverbs* (1546) notes 'Plentie is no deinte, ye see not your owne ease. I see, ye can not see the wood for trees'. Quite. The French version is said to date only from the 20th century, which is odd when one considers the similarity of the expressions ('it is the tree which hides the forest') and the longevity of the English phrase. For interest, the Italian equivalent suggests that one goes to Rome and doesn't see the Pope.

Still waters run deep

Il faut se méfier de l'eau qui dort *(Beware of water which sleeps)*

Too polite by half

Trop poli pour être honnête *(Too polite to be honest)*

To have blinkers on   Porter des œillères

To bark up the wrong tree   Faire fausse route *(To be on the wrong road)*

To have the wool pulled over your eyes
Etre le dindon de la farce

This expression, meaning to be made a fool of, duped or hoodwinked, has an uncertain origin in its French version. The 'dindon' is literally a male turkey, whose very appearance is somewhat foolish, and perhaps this is the origin of the first possible etymology. The 'farce' refers to comic plays or sketches which used to be performed during village fairs in medieval times. These were often based on some poor dupe, the 'dindon', who was taken for a ride by other villainous characters. This use of 'dindon' dates from the end of the 18th century. The other interpretation derives from the Old French meaning of 'dinde' (female turkey) – a naïve, gullible girl. A small linguistic shift and this became 'dindon', with the similar meaning of someone who is easily duped. The 'farce' might refer to 'farcir' (to stuff in a culinary sense) and the notion that someone who has been made a fool of has been well and truly stuffed! Either seems plausible. The English version is more evident. In olden days the wigs, which used to be de rigueur for both sexes, were referred to as wool presumably because they looked like sheep's wool in texture and curls. Thus if you pulled a wig down over someone's eyes, they couldn't see what mischief you were up to. This phrase was in common use by the mid-19th century and probably before, given historical fashion trends.

To let the cat out of the bag
Vendre la mèche

The French version of this expression, meaning to reveal a secret, has an interesting historical basis. 'Mèche', in this context, is the wick or fuse of an explosive device. In the 16th century mines or bombs were charged with such a 'mèche', but could be disarmed by the enemy by 'éventer' (exposing to air) the fuse. Thus the original phrase was 'éventer la mèche', which took on the sense of to discover the basis of a plot. During the 19th century the expression changed to 'vendre', which in its original sense also meant 'to betray' (not just 'to sell'), hence the modern meaning. The English version relates to another phrase, to buy a pig in a poke, which refers to the age-old practice of trying to swindle someone into believing that the living animal concealed in a bag (poke in fact derives from 'poche', which in the Middle Ages meant 'sac' or bag rather than pocket) was a valuable pig. The harsh truth was that it was often a worthless moggie and the unwitting purchaser realised this only when he got home and literally let the cat out of the bag!

Antisocial behaviour
PAS TRÈS SYMPA

To be out of your tree
Fumer la moquette

Who knows where the English version of this expression, meaning to be out of it in an amusing way, usually after the consumption of drugs, comes from? Perhaps you would have had to be out of your tree to think it up! The French expression 'to smoke the carpet' seems equally bizarre and dates from the second half of the 20th century. It could refer either to an association (while stoned) between the fibres of a carpet and the fibres of grass/weed, possibly a reference to hemp as both a textile and a drug. Alternatively, it could imply that smoking synthetic carpet fibres might indeed induce some kind of hallucinogenic state. We suspect that the latter would only end up with a trip to the hospital and is thus best avoided. Note that the French expression can also mean to be generally spaced out without the use of illegal drugs.

To play hooky
Faire l'école buissonnière

...or to bunk off, play truant, deliberately not attend school or indeed the office. Sometimes written 'hookey', the English version probably derives from the Middle English use of 'to hook' or 'to hook it', which meant to run away stealthily – as well you might from an overbearing head teacher. The French version has a number of possible origins. 'Buisson' means bush or shrub, and back in the 1540s schools described thus were found in the countryside. Children of farming families have historically been allowed to be less strict in their school attendance when it is harvest time and all hands possible are required to work in the fields. This is one possible source of the phrase. Another is that at around the same time the primary schools of Paris and its suburbs were reformed to fall under the aegis of the Catholic

Church. Those who didn't subscribe to its teachings preferred their children not to attend these religious schools. Instead they were educated in clandestine, makeshift schools, in the countryside surrounding the capital, to avoid detection. One thing is clear: as long as going to school has been compulsory, non-attendance has been a pastime for many students.

Old habits die hard
Les mauvaises habitudes collent à la peau
(Bad habits stick to the skin)

To be as high as a kite
Etre complètement stone   *(To be completely stoned)*

To smoke like a chimney
Fumer comme un pompier   *(To smoke like a fireman)*

To swear like a trooper   Jurer comme un charretier
(To swear like a carter)

To drag your heels
Traîner les pieds

To be bone idle
Etre fainéant comme une couleuvre
(To be as lazy as a grass snake)

To be a gadfly   Etre la mouche du coche
(To be the fly of the coach)

Spare the rod and spoil the child
Qui aime bien, châtie bien   *(Who loves well, punishes well)*

Not all there

To have lost your marbles
Avoir perdu la boule

In other words, to have gone mad or bonkers. The French is easy to understand; 'boule' (ball) is simply another word for head. The French thus lose their heads when they are mad, or when they are aristocrats living in the wrong century. Equally, you could 'perdre le nord' (lose the north) in the sense of being unable to read a compass when you are disorientated mentally. The origin of the English version is less clear. It would seem to date from the early 20th century and comes possibly from America. Theories about what 'marbles' might refer to stretch from testicles to the Elgin marbles to the children's game. One other suggestion is that 'marbles' is a corruption of the French 'meubles' or furniture, as evidenced in phrases like, 'He hasn't got all his furniture at home'. This idea approximates to the multitude of sayings such as 'not the full picnic' (page 23), which communicate the same idea of being short of or lacking in something, either intelligence or sanity!

To be as mad as a box of frogs
Avoir une araignée au plafond

In other words, to be completely insane. The English version is relatively recent and alludes to the supposed behaviour of an army of frogs if you were to enclose them in a box. They would be hopping around all over the place, in fact they would be hopping mad, hence the expression. The French expression is significantly older, having first been recorded in 1867 and its literal translation – to have a spider in the ceiling – seems close to the English 'batty' version (see 'to have bats in the belfry', overleaf). Indeed, the 'plafond' has long since meant the brain, but the use of 'araignée' is slightly trickier to explain. Perhaps it refers to a room filled with spiders' webs, suggesting a brain that is in disrepair. Alternatively it alludes to the spider's reputation as an undesirable creature, terrifying to arachnophobes and definitely something you wouldn't want running around in your head. Other European nations have similar problems with their 'upper storeys' in their equivalent expressions. The Germans have a damaged roof, the Danish have rats in the attic, while the Portuguese have little monkeys in theirs!

As daft as a brush
Complètement cintré *(Completely curved)*

They think we're a bunch of muppets
Ils nous prennent pour des jambons *(They take us for hams)*

As thick as two short planks
Bête comme ses pieds *(As stupid as your feet)*

She's not the sharpest knife in the drawer
Elle n'a pas inventé le fil à couper le beurre
(She didn't invent the wire to cut the butter)

He's a few beers short of a six-pack
Il n'a pas inventé la poudre *(He didn't invent the powder)*

To have bats in the belfry
Travailler du chapeau

Not a description you'd want to hear applied to someone you fancied dating, since it means to be mad – usually harmless, but insane just the same. The French expression has a number of possible origins. The synonym 'fou comme un chapelier' (as mad as a hatter) gives us a clue, since someone who worked with hats in olden days was exposed to mercury nitrate. This toxic substance, inhaled all day long by milliners, damaged the brain and rendered poor French hat makers mad. Considering the Mad Hatter in *Alice in Wonderland*, it wasn't just the French milliners who were afflicted. Another possible explanation is that in France in the Middle Ages, 'travailler' also meant to be agitated, and 'chapeau' was another word for head. Someone who was worked up in the head was probably mad. The English version has a more obscure origin. There are a number of 18th-century examples of characters with the name Battie or Batty, who were either mad themselves or worked with the insane, but neither of these is a convincing explanation, especially when we add the belfry to the expression. By the early 20th century belfry had come to mean head and the expression existed as the name of a play in the late 1930s. Why bats? Perhaps because they flew around with no apparent purpose or logic. For interest, the Italians are deemed to have crickets in their head when they are mad.

He's not the full picnic
Il n'a pas inventé l'eau tiède *(He didn't invent lukewarm water)*

To have been dropped on your head as a child Avoir été bercé trop près du mur *(To have been rocked too close to the wall)*

To have a screw loose
Avoir un petit vélo dans la tête *(To have a small bicycle in the head)*

As confused as a rabbit caught in the headlights
On dirait une poule qui a trouvé un couteau
(One could say a hen that has found a knife)

To be a complete airhead
Ne rien avoir dans le citron *(To have nothing in the lemon)*

An oddball Un drôle de zèbre *(A strange zebra)*

A queer fish Un drôle d'oiseau *(A strange bird)*

Still wet behind the ears Un petit jeûnot *(A little lad)*

Make an effort!
FAIS UN EFFORT !

Just a big girl's blouse
Vraiment une poule mouillée

Wimp! Wuss! Lightweight! However you might say it, the meaning is the same. The English expression is relatively modern, possibly from the North of England, often used by Australians and generally not too offensive to the male in question. Why it has its current form is unknown, but a blouse is only ever worn by a female and suggests something frilly and possibly floral, while a big girl is as far from being a hunky man as you might get. Put the two together and you have the opposite of macho manhood. The French expression can be used for women, but is usually reserved for men. It refers to how a hen behaves when it has been doused with rain and is thus damp/wet (mouillée)...shivering, hiding, huddling, listless, seemingly unable to fly and thus vulnerable to attack. Far from being modern, this expression dates back to the 17th century.

To be a workshy soap dodger
Avoir un poil dans la main *(To have a hair in your hand)*

He didn't bust a gut
Il ne s'est pas cassé le cul *(He didn't break his arse)*

She doesn't know which way to turn
Elle ne sait plus à quel saint se vouer
(She no longer knows which saint to devote to)

A loafer Un glandeur

A wet rag Une chiffe molle

About as useful as a chocolate teapot
La cinquième roue du carrosse

A veritable disaster for tea-lovers everywhere! What use is a chocolate teapot, since it will surely melt on contact with the boiling water? That is the very sense of the expression: something is of no use whatsoever, similar to 'an ashtray on a motorbike' (below). The English version is modern and can also be found as chocolate fireguard and chocolate kettle. The French version refers back to a means of transport in the 19th century and before. The horse-drawn coach or 'carrosse' was used to carry passengers from A to B. The wheels being made of wood and iron, these were unlikely to puncture as modern rubber tyres do, and so there was no need to have a fifth wheel, 'roue'. This would have been literally a waste of space. The car with pneumatic tyres replaced the coach, and ironically it then did become important to have a spare (ergo fifth) tyre stored in the boot in case of puncture. The expression however has remained in its original form, and a derivation of 'carrosse' is still often seen in 'carrosserie', a car body repair workshop which removes dents or scratches.

It's like an ashtray on a motorbike
C'est un cataplasme sur une jambe de bois

In other words, absolutely no use whatsoever. Anyone who has ever been on a motorbike will know that even at low speeds the wind power is such that everything gets blown around. Any attempt to avoid littering by stubbing out cigarette butts in an open-top ashtray would thus be futile. An English version of the French expression, 'as much use as a poultice on a wooden leg', also exists, but in either language the end result is the same – none. A poultice can be effective only on living flesh or tissue and would have no effect on inanimate matter such as wood, even if it did take the form of a leg. Pirates be warned. The French expression has existed since the 18th century, and indeed the sense of the phrase exists in many languages, futile activities being a human preoccupation. Other nations invoke other objects: the Dutch have butter on the gallows while the Romanians have a suction cup to aid a corpse.

No use to man or beast
Pas un foudre de guerre

Someone like this is no better than a chocolate teapot i.e. completely useless. The English version is self-evident, the French is ironic. In the 17th century, a 'foudre de guerre' (a lightning bolt of war) was a redoubtable warrior or captain, feared and admired. Over time the phrase became someone who wasn't any of these and thus was of no use to anyone.

He can't hold a candle to her
Il ne lui arrive pas à la cheville

In other words, he cannot be compared favourably to her or is inferior to her. The English version dates back to the 16th century in the form 'for' her (or him) rather than 'to' her. This is more logical since the expression derives from the idea that, in the days before electric lighting, a lowly apprentice would be required to hold up a candle so that the more experienced workman could see to do his job. Holding a candle could not be described as skilled labour, so if the lad couldn't even do this, then he definitely compared unfavourably with his superior. Over time the phrase has been used in a wider context and can refer to anyone who is deemed inferior to another. The French version dates from the 18th century. Since the 'cheville' (ankle) is very close to the floor, someone who can't even measure up that high can be seen to be lowly indeed. Interestingly, an older form of the expression invoked 'la ceinture' (belt), implying that it was easier to compare favourably to someone in days of yore than it became in more modern times.

Saving graces
LE BON CÔTÉ DES CHOSES

No flies on him
C'est une fine mouche

In other words, astute, perceptive, possibly even quite cunning. The English version comes to us via cattle ranchers in America and Australia during the 19th century. Flies tend not to be attracted to, or at least stay on, the beasts which were lively. In contrast, the lethargic bovines entice them in their masses. By extension someone who is quick, either of mind or body, could be said to be without flies. The French version dates back to the 15th century, though the word 'mouche' (fly) was in use as early as the late 1300s to mean spy or liar. Flies have many characteristics, not least their ability to observe and yet remain elusive. This is the sense of the French expression – it is someone who is perceptive, but often discreetly so.

She wasn't born yesterday!
Pas folle, la guêpe !

…and so, in the English version, is old enough and wise enough not to be easily fooled. This expression was in common use by the mid-18th century, although the synonyms 'I'm not as green as I am cabbage-looking' and 'I didn't come down in the last shower' are probably more recent. The French version literally translates as 'not mad, the wasp', which seems bizarre since wasps are not known for their (in)sanity. The phrase, from the mid-19th century, was originally 'pas bête, la guêpe', or 'not stupid, the wasp', a play on the dual meaning of 'bête' as 'animal' and 'dumb'. To boot, at the same time, a 'guêpe' was someone smart and wily and it is in this sense that the phrase was used. By the 20th century 'bête' had changed to 'folle', though we don't know exactly why, and has remained so ever since.

As cool as a cucumber
D'un calme olympien

In other words, very calm, unperturbed, unruffled. The English expression dates from at least 1732, when it was cited in a poem by John Gay. Cucumbers were one of the earliest vegetables to be cultivated, along with pumpkins and watermelons, and due to their high moisture content have traditionally had cooling properties. The expression probably derives from a play on the two senses of cool, along with a nice alliteration. The French version, citing an Olympian calm, possibly refers back to Homer, who wrote of the calm to be found on Mount Olympus, where the gods lived in tranquil happiness. Alternatively, it could refer to the comportment of either Zeus (who is claimed by some never to have lost his temper) or more likely to his long-suffering wife Hera, who on more than one occasion was forced to turn a blind eye to her husband's philandering. Cool and calm indeed. Those with a strong view on Gallic infidelity, draw your own conclusion.

He doesn't mince his words
Il n'y va pas par quatre chemins

Thus this is a very direct man, one who gets straight to the point and says what he thinks. The French version dates from the 17th century and implies that there is only one path worth taking to travel in the most effective way from A to B. It is simply a waste of time to try out the other three of the four possibilities. What is true for actions, is true for words. The English expression originates in the 16th century, though at this time existed only in a positive sense. Mincing words had the same effect as mincing meat – the smaller and more numerous the pieces, the easier it would be to digest. By the 19th century, the phrase was negated to give the current meaning. For interest, the Germans don't put a leaf in front of their mouths and the Spanish try not to get lost in the branches while going straight for the grain in their equivalent expressions.

To hold all the trumps Avoir tous les atouts dans son jeu
(To have all the trumps in your game)

I didn't come down in the last shower
Je ne suis pas tombé de la dernière pluie

As good as gold Sage comme une image *(As good as an image)*

The patience of a saint Une patience d'ange *(The patience of an angel)*

A clever monkey Malin comme un singe

As cunning as a fox Rusé comme un renard

The salt of the earth Bon comme le pain *(As good as the bread)*

To live life to the full
Mener la vie tambour battant *(To live life banging a drum)*

To be all sweetness and light
Etre tout sucre, tout miel *(To be all sugar, all honey)*

To have mended your ways
Etre rangé des voitures *(To be tidied up of cars)*

He doesn't fart around Il ne peigne pas le cou de la girafe
(He doesn't comb the neck of the giraffe)

To paddle your own canoe
Mener sa barque tout seul *(To lead your boat alone)*

To know the score Connaître la musique *(To know the music)*

As snug as a bug in a rug
Comme un coq en pâte

In other words, to be very comfortable indeed, often implying you are tucked in somewhere warm and cosy. The French expression, which dates back to the 16th century, has an additional sense of being well looked after and at ease, for which the English might also say 'like pigs in clover'. Originally the French was 'comme un coq en panier' (like a cockerel in a basket), referring to the snug fit of the basket in which the bird was taken to market. By the 17th century 'panier' had become 'pâte', which means either dough/pastry or a pie itself. Arguably, this is a less agreeable situation for the cockerel to find itself in! And yet the French version is not used in an ironic sense – the Gallic cockerel is happy and well! The English dates from the 18th century, although snug existed as a type of parlour room in an inn for many years before then. Many attribute the first use of this expression to Benjamin Franklin, but there is evidence of its being used earlier. In a less appealing fashion the Germans invoke maggots in bacon fat in their expression with a similar meaning.

To have the luck of the Irish
Avoir le cul bordé de nouilles (!)

To be incredibly lucky or fortunate, though you might not necessarily believe it on first glance at either of these expressions. The French version literally translates as 'He has noodles around his arse', which doesn't seem a particularly pleasant or lucky condition to be in. At least since the start of the 20th century 'avoir du cul' has meant to be lucky, as do '…du pot' and '…du bol' – both of which are words dating from the 19th century which also mean arse. While 'cul' is a little vulgar in modern French, it hasn't always been so, if we consider harmless examples such as 'cul-de-sac'. However, even if you accept that 'to have some ass' is lucky, why on earth should it be bordered with noodles? One source suggests this comes from Marseille, home of the tall story and exaggeration, and geographically close to Italy. Noodles are a form of pasta and it seems some lively lad in the 1930s accessorised the existing expression with noodles and it stuck. There is another possible explanation involving prison and haemorrhoids (which we will spare you). Moving on. The sense of the English expression appears to be ironic, since it is difficult – considering unwanted foreign occupation, potato famines and civil war – to claim that the Irish have had a particularly lucky history. The expression probably refers to leprechauns; mythical Irish fairies who live in the hedgerows, repair shoes and hide crocks of gold at the end of the rainbow. If captured by a human, they will grant you three wishes in order to be set free, hence the element of good luck... but you must keep hold of the wily creature, otherwise he will run away before you can say 'Jack Robinson'.

Don't forget to check the answers to the quiz.
See how many you got right ...

1. Small fry
2. To be not the sharpest knife in the drawer
3. As stiff as a board
4. To be bone idle
5. A cock-and-bull story
6. As good as gold
7. To be a scaredy cat
8. All sweetness and light

a) Un second couteau
b) Ne pas avoir inventé le fil à couper le beurre
c) Souple comme un verre de lampe
d) Etre fainéant comme une couleuvre
e) Une histoire à dormir debout
f) Sage comme une image
g) Avoir froid aux yeux
h) Tout sucre, tout miel

THE RELATIONSHIP GAME
RELATIONS, MODE D'EMPLOI

HUMAN RELATIONS ARE TRICKY ENOUGH WITHOUT THE ADDED PROBLEMS OF A LANGUAGE BARRIER. How to express the right degree of disagreement or togetherness? What to say when relationships go wrong and, most importantly, how to communicate in the language of love? We don't have the answers to the mating game here, sadly, but we can do our best to give you the right idioms to give it a go in another language!

Agree to disagree?
IL VA Y AVOIR DU RIFIFI

To give someone the rough side of your tongue
Passer un savon à quelqu'un

Or to give someone a telling off, a reprimand or a rebuke. The date and origin of the English expression are unknown, but it possibly came to exist in opposition to being smooth-tongued or, in its earliest incarnation (1599), a 'Smoothboots', which meant a flatterer. To get the rough side of the tongue thus was to receive harsh words. The French version is more obscure. Why should 'passing a soap' to someone mean telling them off? It's actually a development of a 17th-century phrase 'laver la tête (à quelqu'un)' or 'to wash someone's head', which meant to hit or beat someone, and eventually to reprimand them. At this time, pre-washing machines, all laundry was done at the communal fountain where village women would gather to wash and gossip using soap and a large wooden beater/rod to get their whites clean. The expression for a rebuke evolved from washing to include soap at the start of the 18th century and now le savon can be passed ('passé'), given ('donné') or taken ('pris'), according to the situation. Interestingly, the Italians and Germans still use the equivalent of a 'head-washing' to mean a telling-off. The Greeks on the other hand sing hymns to someone...

To bad-mouth someone
Casser du sucre sur le dos de quelqu'un

...is to speak badly of someone, slander them, muck rake or backbite, usually in their absence. The English phrase comes to us via American slang, and though its meaning is clear, its date of origin is unknown. The French expression is altogether more interesting, since the literal translation 'to break sugar on the back of someone' hints at an interesting etymology. In fact, to understand the origin of this 19th-century phrase we need to divide it into two parts. At the time sugar was still a luxury item and was sold in small loaves (ingots, perhaps?) which had to be broken into small crumbs before they could be used. 'Casser' had another meaning aside from 'to break' – it was also to reveal unpleasant secrets about someone. These two facts explain the first part of the idiom. The second part suggests the metaphoric weight of the slander and/or that their back is turned or they are not present when the malicious words are spoken.

To shout blue murder
Gueuler comme un putois

This is an interesting example of how language changes over time. The English expression derives from the French expletive 'Morbleu', short for 'mort bleu', which itself was a way of saying 'Mort Dieu' (God's death) without blaspheming. This substitution of 'bleu' for 'Dieu' still exists in the exclamation 'Sacrebleu !', though apart from Inspector Clouseau no self-respecting Frenchman would ever say it, at least not in public. For the English, the polecat ('putois') is invoked more for its perceived sexual appetite ('randy as a....') than its vocal cords. But although generally a quiet animal it is known for emitting a piercing shriek when scared or in danger and it is this that the French refer to. Like its skunk cousin, it is also known to let off a very unpleasant odour, but the less said about that the better...

Handbags at dawn
Un crêpage de chignon

...is a cat-fight, not between two moggies, but rather between two women or even two 'queens'. The idea behind both the English and the French expressions is that no real damage is inflicted by either party; it is more a war of words, with some posturing and perhaps hair pulling and scratching, than anything more serious. The English version is a play on the age-old duelling tradition, when the insulted party would 'demand satisfaction' by challenging the perceived offender to an early-morning confrontation known as 'pistols at dawn'. The handbag, the weapon of choice for the modern woman, is a particularly weighty item given all that is schlepped around within. Thus it is armed with handbags rather than firearms that women duel. The French expression, frizzing or messing up the chignon, has an equally pejorative sense to it, suggesting that ruining someone's hairstyle is the worst that can happen to two women who disagree. Those with carefully coiffed locks who find themselves in dispute with a 'bonne femme' in France have been warned.

To take the wind out of someone's sails
Couper l'herbe sous le pied

...is to burst their bubble, to thwart or discourage them. The English version is a naval expression which arises from the fact that if one sailing boat gets upwind of another it can steal or block the wind getting to the sails of the other. The obstructed boat loses speed as the sails simply flap about. It is a tactic often used in dinghy racing. The French version is similar to another English expression, 'to cut the ground from under somebody's feet', though the French seems to specify that this ground consists of grass. In fact, the expression dates back to the 16th century, at which time 'herbe' had the wider meaning of any vegetable or herb whose leaves were edible. Thus the sense of the expression is to harvest someone else's food supply, a more serious problem than simply mowing their lawn. For interest, the Italians steal someone else's shoes in their equivalent expression.

A storm in a tea cup
Une tempête dans un verre d'eau

Given that the English are known to be a nation of tea drinkers, it is no surprise to find references to tea in many expressions. It is however a surprise to discover that the meaning of this expression – a big fuss about relatively little – dates back as far as the Roman statesman and writer Cicero (52 BC), though he was less bothered with tea cups and more concerned with waves in his wine ladle. And given that the French have the honour of being the world's greatest wine consumers, it is also a surprise that their expression should be abstemious to the point of being teetotal – or should that be tea-total? It is relatively recent, with its first recorded use only in the mid-19th century.

To slag someone off
Habiller quelqu'un pour l'hiver *(To dress someone for winter)*

To send someone away with a flea in their ear
Mettre la puce à l'oreille de quelqu'un

To get a dressing-down
Recevoir une volée de bois vert *(To receive a volley of green wood)*

To have a sharp tongue Avoir la dent dure *(To have the hard tooth)*

His wife showed him the yellow card
Sa femme lui a donné un carton jaune

Say what?
CAUSE TOUJOURS

A little bird told me
Mon petit doigt me l'a dit

This expression refers to a secret source of information whose identity the speaker is loath to reveal. The English almost certainly derives from the Bible, *Ecclesiastes 10:20* to be precise, though it is worth pointing out that birds have acted as messengers for many years and still do in the form of carrier pigeons. The French expression dates from at least the 17th century and possibly earlier. The name for the little finger in French is 'l'auriculaire' and those with a grounding of Latin will recognise the root auricular, which lends itself to a varied number of expressions regarding hearing/ears/witnessing etc. Alternatively, it could be called thus because it is the finger most commonly used (by Frenchmen) to clean out their ears! Joking aside, it is the little finger which serves to whisper secrets to the French ear.

The jungle telegraph
Le téléphone arabe

Both expressions refer to a means of quickly spreading information, often rumours, usually via word of mouth. The English version exists in many forms – the Australian bush telegraph and the American grapevine to name but two. We prefer the jungle telegraph which implies beating of tom-tom drums and relays of runners to share information between tribes living in the deepest, darkest subtropical vegetation. Unlike the Anglophone expressions, which date from the 19th century, the French appeared only in the first half of the 20th. Its origin is historic and refers to France's former colonies in North Africa. At the time, these Arab countries were very much developing states and so, since the modern telephonic technology had yet to be fully installed, information still circulated by word of mouth. Interestingly, the phrase bush telegraph or 'telephone de brousse' also exists in French, though here the bush referred to is (French colonial) Central African rather than Australian.

His bark is worse than his bite   Il aboie plus qu'il ne mord

We're not on first-name terms
On n'a pas gardé les cochons ensemble   *(We haven't kept pigs together)*

I have no say in the matter
Je n'ai pas voix au chapitre   *(I have no voice in the chapter)*

Let's talk turkey   Parlons franc   *(Let's talk frank)*

A trouser call
Un coup de fil involontaire   *(An unintentional phone call)*

Speak of the devil and he's sure to appear
Quand on parle du loup, on en voit sa queue
(When one speaks of the wolf, one sees his tail)

To cry wolf   Crier au loup

We're in this together
D'ACCORD

To get on like a house on fire
S'entendre comme larrons en foire

To find a kindred spirit or to have a good understanding with someone. The English expression probably dates back to the 17th century, specifically to the Great Fire of London in 1666, but this is only a hypothesis. One of the main reasons why this fire, which reportedly destroyed 70,000 of the City's 80,000 homes, was so destructive was that the houses were built of wood and were crammed in close together. With the wind pushing the fire, it was unfortunately all too easy for flames to leap from house to house, destroying them in a very short time. The French expression dates from the same era. The 'larron' (knave/scoundrel) was a petty thief who would often steal wallets, using an accomplice (hence the use of the plural 'larrons') to distract the hapless victim while his pocket was picked. The addition of 'foire' or fair came later and meant an agricultural or large social gathering as opposed to a funfair. Over time, the expression lost its allusion to criminal activity and took on its current meaning of two people getting on well together, if sometimes up to no good.

As thick as thieves
Comme cul et chemise

The English version of this expression, which means to be very close to someone, often acting in collusion, dates from at least the early 19th century. It derives from the idea that those who are plotting something often use a language or dialect that only they understand to avoid detection by others. This used to be known as 'thieves' Latin'. While you might think that certain thieves were stupid, the sense of 'thick' here is not of intelligence, rather to be closely set or knit. The French expression is even older, dating from the 17th century, and has sartorial roots. The original form was 'être deux culs dans une chemise' ('to be two bottoms in one shirt', and therefore obviously very close together). Over time this evolved to its current format, which refers to the proximity between a person and their clothes, but the meaning is the same: two people who share this intimacy, in a completely asexual manner, are deemed to be complicit.

To be hand in glove
Etre copains comme cochons *(To be friends like pigs)*

Birds of a feather flock together
Qui se ressemble, s'assemble *(Those who look alike gather together)*

There is honour among thieves
Les loups ne se mangent pas entre eux
(Wolves don't eat each other)

In the same boat
Logés à la même enseigne

Not necessarily a happy situation in which to find yourself, since it implies that you will undergo the same (difficult) conditions as someone else. The English version probably dates from the mid-19th century, though some say the 16th. Its origins could even go back as far as Cicero and the phrase *in eadem es navi*, written in a letter around 53 BC. The idea is clear: if the sea is rough, we will both get seasick; if the boat sinks, we will both drown. The French version dates from the late 18th century and translates literally as 'living at or under the same sign'. This is a reference to the signs which used to hang outside shops to announce their trade or wares. The sense is that two shopkeepers in the same line of trade will suffer the same business woes.

A different kettle of fish
Une autre paire de manches

In other words, something completely different, as are these expressions in their respective languages. The English version is probably Scottish in origin, with 'kettle' referring to a metal cooking pot for outdoor use in which salmon were cooked. References to kettles of fish can be found from the mid-18th century, although the expression then mentioned a 'pretty' or 'fine' kettle and meant a mess or a tricky situation, as it still does. Not until the 20th century can we find a record of the development of the phrase to 'a different kettle' and its current meaning. The French version dates back to the start of the 16th century and refers to the custom of having garments with removable sleeves (manches). This was highly practical since it meant you could simply change the sleeves of your dress and appear to have a completely new outfit at a much lower cost. On a less practical note, these removable sleeves also became tokens of affection and a proof of fidelity between lovers. The French phrase is also now used to refer to a new start or new task, which is not only completely different to the precedent, but also more difficult.

To give someone a lot of rope
Lâcher la bride à quelqu'un *(To release the bridle to someone)*

Arm in arm
Bras dessus, bras dessous *(Arm above, arm underneath)*

To meet someone half way
Couper la poire en deux *(To cut the pear in two)*

To blow one's own trumpet
S'envoyer des fleurs *(To send yourself flowers)*

Affairs of the heart
SORTEZ LES VIOLONS

To be the apple of someone's eye
Etre la prunelle des yeux de quelqu'un

This expression, meaning something or someone that is held very dear, is a good example of the differences between French and English. In Saxon times, the 'apple' of the eye was the pupil, and was correctly deemed critical to one's vision. Over time the expression came to have its current metaphorical meaning. The French see things differently. 'Prunelle' is a diminutive of 'prune' (plum) and was used for the pupil of the eye as early as the 12th century. Even though the modern word 'pupille' had been introduced by the start of the 14th century, the idiom, which dates from the same period, held on to 'prunelle'. Different fruits, different languages, same meaning.

To make sheep's eyes at someone
Regarder quelqu'un avec des yeux de merlan frit

Neither of these expressions, which mean to give amorous, lovesick glances at an object of affection, strikes us as being particularly romantic. Sheep are not known for their good looks or sparkling eyes, and to the best of our knowledge aren't great flirts either. The idea of the expression, which apparently dates back to the early 16th century, is that a sheep's eye is unblinking, shows lots of the white and fixes in a languishing way on the object it observes. We are not convinced. The French expression isn't much better, since we move from sheep to fish, specifically to the eyes of a fried whiting. Truly the language of love. The expression derives from the observation that a fish eye, in this case whiting, will bulge from its socket when cooked and take on a white opaque colour... similar to when a person rolls their eyes to the heavens and you see only the white. In silent movies, this exaggerated rolling of the eyes was used to symbolise being love-struck and the expression has remained.

To make puppy-dog eyes at someone
Faire les yeux doux à quelqu'un *(To make sweet eyes at someone)*

Faint heart never won fair lady
Jamais couard n'aura belle amie
(A coward will never have a beautiful girlfriend)

He's only human
Il n'est pas de bois *(He isn't made of wood)*

I wouldn't touch him with a barge-pole
Il me débecte *(He disgusts me)*

To find your soulmate Trouver l'âme sœur *(To find your sister soul)*

Every Jack has his Jill
Chaque casserole a son couvercle *(Each saucepan has its lid)*

To play gooseberry
Tenir la chandelle

A sorry state of events. When you find yourself a sad singleton out with a couple, you are playing gooseberry or 'holding the candle', as the French expression literally translates. Of the two, arguably the French is the more unpalatable. It dates back to the start of the 19th century, in the days before electricity and bedside table lights. Some poor valet or lady's maid would have to stand holding a candle in his or her master/mistress's bedroom so that the amorous couple could see what they were doing while they performed their conjugal duties. That the servants' backs would be turned to the action is of small comfort, since ear plugs would not have been provided. The English gooseberry seems a more enjoyable role and derives from gooseberry-picker. In the 19th century this was another name for a chaperone, who presumably occupied herself ostensibly gathering fruit while her charges whispered sweet nothings to each other. At the time, a chaperone was essential to the reputation of any young lady, and was almost always a woman. Nowadays the term in English is used more for an unwanted third party of either sex who tags along. Still, better that than a French candlelight voyeur!

A mid-life crisis
Le démon de midi
....

If a male friend or relative over the age of 40 suddenly buys a leather jacket and/or a motorbike and starts flirting with girls young enough to be his daughter, he is probably suffering from this. This social 'disease' afflicts those caught between youth and old age, and is a fear of growing old or a sensation that life is passing one by too quickly. There is, thankfully, a cure, but it can take a few years and (with hindsight) some ridiculous behaviour to get there. The term midlife crisis has existed in English since the early 19th century, but the concept has probably existed since Adam. The French version invokes the idea of the *daemonius meridianus* or 'diable méridien' – the devil who tempts man during daylight hours (as opposed to the devil who works nights). These temptations could include anything unholy, but by the 17th century this particular devil had come to refer specifically to temptations of the flesh, 'le démon de la chair'. Perhaps the experience of middle-aged men lusting after young girls in an attempt to recapture their youth provoked the link in French between 'midi' (which means midday, as does 'méridien') and someone who is in the middle of their expected lifespan...and arguably ought to know better!

To find the perfect match
Trouver chaussure à son pied

When this happens, Cupid's bow has hit the target, you have found the yin to your yang, a match made in heaven or the perfect partner (or solution depending on the context). The French version, to find a shoe for one's foot, dates from the early 17th century. Its meaning would be clear to anyone who has had to hobble around in ill-fitting shoes: finding a perfect fit is a blessing. However, the French also has an erotic undertone to it, since 'prendre son pied' means to have sexual pleasure, and so the imagery of the foot slipping into the shoe might be less Cinderella and Prince Charming than it seems!

✄

A sugar daddy   Un vieux richard   *(An old rich man)*

A toy boy   Un gigolo

To be a cougar
Aimer la viande fraîche   *(To like fresh meat)*

A babe magnet   Un aspirateur à gonzesses   *(A girl hoover)*

A trophy wife   Une femme trophée

A stag night
Un enterrement de vie de garcon   *(A burial of the life as a boy)*

A hen night
Un enterrement de vie de jeune fille
(A burial of the life as an unmarried girl)

To tie the knot
Se mettre la corde au cou   *(To put the rope around your neck)*

The ball and chain   La rombière   *(The regular)*

My better half   Ma moitié   *(My half)*

You can't live on love alone   On ne peut pas vivre d'amour et d'eau
fraîche   *(You can't live on love and cold water)*

✄

To fall in love at the drop of a hat
Avoir un cœur d'artichaut

Said of someone who is constantly in and out of love with different people: in short, fickle. The English version is not restricted to falling in love. You can do anything at the drop of a hat, a phrase which has existed since the 1850s and possibly refers to the action being used to mark the start of an unofficial fight or contest. Perhaps because the English are not a nation known for wooing and amorous prowess, there is no direct equivalent of 'the heart of an artichoke' which the French invoke. The artichoke is not chosen for any perceived properties or benefits, rather for its form, since its heart is surrounded by multiple layers of leaves. The idea of the expression is 'une feuille pour tout le monde', or a leaf for everyone, specifically each person loved. Ah, l'amour…

When relationships go wrong
AMES EN PEINE

To be stood up
Se faire poser un lapin

A sorry condition to find yourself in, since this means that your date hasn't turned up, leaving you with only your humiliation for company. The English version does not have a convincing history, though it would seem originally to have been American and to date from the early 20th century. Whether one was left with a gap in the dance card, waiting at the bus stop, the bar, the train station – who knows? The French version is more colourful. In the 19th century 'faire poser' was another way of saying 'faire attendre' (to make wait), and 'un lapin' was a form of payment. Thus 'poser un lapin' was to fail to pay a lady of the night for services rendered. Over time this expression came to mean not keeping an obligation or promise until by the 20th century it had taken on its current meaning. At least we know the origin now, even if it might not soften the blow of the occurrence.

To cry your heart out
Pleurer comme une Madeleine

Woe, he or she who cries so much since they must be in floods of tears. The English expression is easy to understand, even if its date of origin is unknown. You are crying so hard that you think your heart will explode from your body, that you are being wrung dry with the effort of crying. Perhaps it also refers to the fact that affairs of the heart tend to make one cry particularly violently. The French version initially appears more obscure, as the most famous madeleine (small sponge cake) probably belongs to Marcel Proust. In his early 20th-century epic *A la recherche du temps perdu*, the mere taste of such a cake evokes specific and involuntary memories from the narrator's past. However, the origin of the expression is less culinary and more biblical: the 'Madeleine' is Marie-Madeleine or Mary Magdalene, who was said to have washed the feet of Jesus with her copious tears after confessing her sins. Originally, in the Middle Ages, the expression for sobbing was 'faire sa Madeleine', which by the start of the 19th century had taken on its current form.

Once bitten, twice shy
Chat échaudé craint l'eau froide

This expression, meaning that you should learn from your experience or that your behaviour is influenced by what has happened to you in the past, has very old roots. The French version, that a scalded cat is scared of cold water, dates from the 13th century, though at this time the poor feline was simply afraid of water; the temperature part was added later. The idea behind the expression is clear:

having had a nasty experience with boiling water, the cat is wary of all water, even the cold stuff which shouldn't do it any harm. The English version is a little more modern, probably dating from the 19th century, with the idea that only an idiot would allow themselves to be bitten twice by the same dog, though a similar expression can be found as far back as Richard Taverner's *Proverbs* of 1545. Interestingly, the Romanians also play on the idea of being scalded, though in their expression he who has been burned by the hot soup blows to cool down his yogurt.

All's fair in love and war
En amour comme à la guerre tous les coups sont permis
(In love as in war all blows are allowed)

Sick at heart
Malheureux comme les pierres *(Unhappy like the stones)*

Out of sight, out of mind
Loin des yeux, loin du cœur *(Far from the eyes, far from the heart)*

There are plenty more fish in the sea
Une de perdue, dix de retrouvées *(One lost, ten found again)*

There is a bad apple in every barrel
Il y a toujours une brebis galeuse dans le troupeau
(There is always one sheep with scabies in the flock)

Lucky in cards, unlucky in love…
Heureux au jeu, malheureux en amour…

As welcome as a fart in a spacesuit
Comme un chien dans un jeu de quilles

A good example of relations breaking down, since this means to be very unwelcome or out of place. The English expression exists in a number of more genteel versions: 'a skunk at a tea party', 'a dog on a putting green', 'a pork chop at a Jewish wedding, to name but a few. Memorably said by a famous Scottish comedian on live TV, the version we have chosen is so evocative, not only of something undesirable, but also of something that lingers substantially longer than one would wish! The French equivalent also invokes a dog interrupting a sporting activity, this time a game of skittles, and dates from the 18th century. One can imagine the chaos as Fido or Médor (his French counterpart) charges around knocking down the nine-pins. Note that you can also be as welcome as a hair in the soup, 'comme un cheveu dans la soupe', in France.

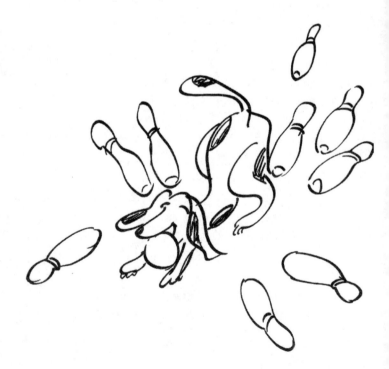

Revenge is sweet
LA VENGANCE EST UN PLAT QUI SE MANGE FROID

Two can play at that game
A bon chat, bon rat

In other words, the same tactics or strategy used by an adversary can be easily used against him or her. The etymology of the English version is unknown, and it is unclear which game was being referred to in the original usage. Walter Scott, in his novel *Woodstock* (1826), seemed to believe it was wrestling, but this may just be one interpretation. The sense of the French version dates back as far as the 16th century, though it has probably existed in the current form only since the 17th, as evidenced in Paul Scarron's *Jodelet* (1645). It possibly refers to an ancient French proverb, 'payer en chats et en rats', which meant to use dud money. This has evolved into 'monkey money' in modern French: 'payer en monnaie de singe'.

There will be hell to pay Ça va chier des bulles *(That will crap bubbles)*

Tit for tat Un prêté pour un rendu *(One borrowed for one given back)*

To screw someone over
Chier dans les bottes de quelqu'un *(To crap in someone's boots)*

To pay someone back in spades
Rendre la monnaie de sa pièce à quelqu'un
(To give someone back the change from their coin)

If you play with fire, you get burned
Qui s'y frotte s'y pique *(Who rubs there, is stung there)*

To rub salt into the wound
Remuer le couteau dans la plaie *(To move the knife in the wound)*

QUIZ ANSWERS

Don't forget to check the answers to the quiz.
See how many you got right . . .

1. To get a dressing-down
2. He's only human
3. A babe magnet
4. To tie the knot
5. We're not on first-name terms

6. There are plenty more fish in the sea
7. There is a bad apple in every barrel

a) Recevoir une volée de bois vert
b) Il n'est pas de bois
c) Un aspirateur à gonzesses
d) Se mettre la corde au cou
e) On n'a pas gardé les cochons ensemble
f) Une de perdue, dix de retrouvées
g) Il y a toujours une brebis galeuse dans le troupeau

THE BEAST WITH TWO BACKS
LA BÊTE À DEUX DOS

I T ALWAYS COMES DOWN TO SEX IN THE END. Even if the actions are the same the world over, the words to describe them are not. To avoid embarrassment before, during or after the event, the following should help.

(!) This chapter comes with a strong health warning and nearly all of the expressions should not be used out of context!

On heat!
EN CHALEUR !

To be a horny devil
Etre un chaud lapin

This expression, which means to be sexually excited or lecherous, has existed in its English form for many decades. The devil has always been the source of temptation and wrongdoing (given that lust is one of the original seven deadly sins), whereas the 'horn' has been associated with the male erection for obvious physical reasons since at least the early 18th century. The horn used to imply adultery and still does in Italy, where 'fare le corne' (to do the horns) means to cuckold someone, usually the husband. This sense has been lost in modern English.

The French expression is slightly more scientific and refers to the well-known predilection of rabbits for procreating. The addition of the adjective 'chaud' or hot is a reference to when animals are in heat and thus have a primeval urge to copulate. The two terms together suggest an almost insatiable sexual appetite...and one unsuspecting Rosbif females might do well to avoid...

The morning glory
Le barreau du matin   *(The morning rung)*

The dawn horn
La gaule du matin   *(The morning pole/rod)*

To be horny
Avoir le feu aux fesses   *(To have fire in your buttocks)*

To get an eyeful
Se rincer l'œil   *(To rinse your eye)*

To put it about a bit
Avoir la cuisse légère   *(To have a light thigh)*

She's got the decorators in
Les Anglais ont débarqués

This euphemism for having your monthly period or the curse is not for ladies (or gents) of a sensitive disposition. The English expression is easily understood if you assume that the decorators use only red paint. The French is based on historical fact. After Napoleon's defeat at Waterloo in 1815, the British disembarked ('débarquer') and occupied France for a further five years. At the time the uniform of the British Army was red and so the French were subject to a sea of red spreading across their country as the soldiers took up their posts. For disgruntled French citizens, associating the flow of one unwelcome red matter with another was easy and possibly rather gratifying!

She's on the rag Elle a ses ours *(She has her bears)*

To have wandering hands
Avoir les mains baladeuses

To goose someone Mettre la main au panier de quelqu'un
(To put your hand in someone's basket)

A skirt-chaser
Un coureur de jupon *(A petticoat runner)*

To have a mind like a sewer
Avoir l'esprit mal tourné *(To have a badly turned mind)*

To go like a barn door in the wind
Etre un bon coup *(To be a good blow)*

To go like a train
Etre chaude comme la braise *(To be hot like the embers)*

Open-minded
OUVERT D'ESPRIT

A friend with benefits
Un ami-amant
....
The modern solution to the problem of busy working lives, with no time for a committed relationship, but still plenty of carnal desires to be fulfilled. Applicable to both men and women, and also known by the name of its more vulgar twin 'fuck-buddy', this is a relationship that is platonic, but sexual at the same time. The 'benefits' are a euphemism for having sex. Popularised by TV and film, the concept, and practice, have become mainstream. Finding a French equivalent is tricky – not that there aren't French

friends who have sex without being 'a couple', just perhaps that there isn't a widely known word for it. 'Ami-amant' seems to cover both aspects while having a much nicer sound than the English 'buddy' version, even if the idea is the same.

AC/DC
A voile et à vapeur

The English version of this expression, meaning bisexual, almost certainly comes to us from the USA. The AC (alternating current) and DC (direct current) were two distinct electric power distribution methods proposed in the late 1880s by two factions led by Westinghouse and Edison respectively. This 'war of the currents' was eventually won by the AC camp, but DC power still exists and many appliances have the capacity to run on either AC or DC by means of a converter. Amateur physics aside, the point here is that to be AC/DC is to have the ability to be two different things at the same time. The origin of the French expression is unknown. Some theories relate the use of a naval term (under sail and steam) to mean bisexuality to the idea that at sea (as in prison) different social norms apply to relationships between men and women. Other more convincing suggestions refer to the introduction of steam as a means of direct power for boats at a time when the same vessel also navigated under sail. Two different propulsions in the same body, the link is easy to imply, whatever the original language.

A chutney ferret (!) De la jaquette *(Of the morning coat)*

A rug muncher (!) Une colleuse de timbres *(A licker of stamps)*

To swing both ways Etre bique et bouc
(To be Billy and Nanny goat)

They are swingers Ils sont échangistes *(They are swappers)*

Single-player game
PLAISIRS SOLITAIRES

To choke the chicken (!)
Se tirer sur l'élastique *(To pull on one's rubber band)*

To spank the monkey (!)
S'astiquer la colonne *(To polish one's column)*

To play pocket billiards (!)
Se gratter les valseuses *(To scratch your waltzers)*

To flick the bean (!)
Jouer de la mandoline *(To play the mandolin)*

On the job
DANS LE FEU DE L'ACTION

To get lucky
Passer à la casserole

This phrase, which means to have sex, needs a little explanation in the French version ('to go over to the saucepan'). It can mean to die, or for a woman to be obliged to have sex (often with her boss or superior) or to lose her virginity…none of which have much to do with luck. However, it can also be used by girls in the same sense of to get laid: 'Si j'ai de la chance, je passerai à la casserole ce soir' and also by boys: 'Si je l'invite au dîner, elle va passer à la casserole.' In the same context the English (gentle) man might say, 'If I buy her dinner, I might get my leg over.' Quite.

To dip your wick (!)
Tremper son biscuit

An almost exclusively male euphemism for having sex. You might not dunk your digestive in your cup of tea in the same way again on realising that the French male 'gets his biscuit wet' when he is playing hide the sausage. The expression dates from the middle of the 20th century, but is a play on 'tremper son pain au pot' which is found in Rabelais' writings back in the 16th century. The 'biscuit' probably derives from the Latin *biscotos*, meaning cooked twice, since the Italians also wet their biscotto when they have sex. The Spanish prefer to wet their 'churro'. The English version (probably also from the mid-20th century) plays on the Cockney rhyming slang 'Hampton Wick', meaning prick or penis.

To hide the sausage (!)
Mettre le petit Jésus dans la crèche *(To put little Jesus in the crib)*

To be in your birthday suit
Etre à poil *(To be naked, literally at hair)*

To give a blow job (!) Tailler une pipe *(To sharpen a pipe)*

You don't have to buy the cow to drink a glass of milk
Pas besoin de lui mettre la bague au doigt pour tirer un coup
(You don't need to put a ring on her finger to pull a hit)

Doggie style (!) En levrette *(In greyhound bitch position)*

You don't have to look at the mantelpiece while stoking the fire
En levrette on ne voit pas sa tête
(In greyhound bitch one doesn't see the head)

A quickie Une sieste crapuleuse *(A villainous siesta)*

A bump-n-run
Un cinq à sept
....

In the age of fast food, it is perhaps not surprising to find expressions in both languages for a fast…ahem…fornication. The English expression is perhaps more graphic, conjuring images of an almost accidental collision of bodies and then a hasty exit, perhaps while hopping to tug on the trouser-legs. So much for true love. The French version, however, has a historical basis which is actually English. At the start of the 19th century the Duchess of Bedford created the concept of afternoon tea, usually served at five o'clock. This practice found its way across the Channel, initially taking the form of a high-society reception between 5 and 7 p.m.; then, at the start of the 20th century, it became less of a public spectacle and more a private assignation, as something (illicit) to do between the end of working day and the return to the family home. It is not explicit in the French expression that the activity should last for the whole two hours, but perhaps the Gallic male pride would prefer us to think that it does!

The after-effects
DÉGÂTS COLLATÉRAUX

The Big 'O'
La petite mort
....

A climax or orgasm. The English version merely highlights that it is something important or worth achieving and thus is referred to as a capital letter only. The French version has a much more interesting history. The expression, the little death, was known in the 16th century, a time of great scientific advances in anatomy and surgery. At this time, it was used to refer to fainting, a temporary black-out or a nervous shaking rather than anything more pleasurable. Presumably, over time, the link was made between the temporary abandonment of consciousness (though not in an auto-erotic sense) and simply falling unconscious, and the 'petite mort' took on its modern meaning.

To have a bun in the oven
Avoir un polichinelle dans le tiroir

What few self-respecting schoolgirls want to hear, since this euphemistic expression means to be pregnant. The French version has a surprisingly cultural history, since Polichinelle is a French version of Pulcinella, a puppet character in the 16th-century Italian commedia dell'arte. Our very own Punch, from Punch and Judy puppet shows, is based on the same character. The root of Pulcinella is *pulcino*, which means chick or baby bird; this makes the expression a little easier to understand: she has a chick (hidden) in the drawer. Why the secret should be hidden in a drawer is unknown. Interestingly 'un secret de Polichinelle' is a badly kept secret and indeed no pregnancy can remain hidden for ever. Eventually, the chick will be will out of the drawer (or is that the cat out of bag?). The origin of the English expression is equally uncertain, with the first plausible literary reference found in the mid-20th century. Aside from the obvious allusion to things taking time to form and develop in a warm place, there is little else to explain how or why Anglophone women gestate buns. As an aside, 'up the duff' is another reference to being pregnant, where duff is a type of boiled pudding, but again the origin is unknown.

The French disease   La chtouille   *(syphilis)*

Don't forget to check the answers to the quiz.
See how many you got right...

1. The dawn horn
2. To goose someone
3. To play pocket billiards
4. You don't have to look at the mantelpiece while stoking the fire
5. To hide the sausage
6. To swing both ways

a) La gaule du matin
b) Mettre la main au panier de quelqu'un
c) Se gratter les valseuses
d) En levrette on ne voit pas sa tête
e) Mettre le petit Jésus dans la crèche
f) Etre bique et bouc

BODY LANGUAGE
LE LANGAGE CORPOREL

BEAUTY IS IN THE EYE OF THE BEHOLDER but sometimes it needs to be communicated too. How to express this in French? This chapter includes ways of describing appearances of all shapes and sizes, as well as phrases for basic bodily functions.

(!) Be warned that the section 'Toilet Humour' comes with a health warning!

Match the following French expressions with their English equivalent. Find the answers at the end of the chapter, if you have the legs to make it that far...

1. Haut comme trois pommes

2. Etre un thon

3. Avoir une tête de crapaud

4. Avoir roulé sa bosse

5. Avoir la courante

6. Un pantalon moulant l'abricot

7. Dégueuler

a) To have a face like a bulldog chewing a wasp

b) Knee high to a grasshopper

c) To look like the back end of a bus

d) To do a technicolour yawn

e) To have been around the block a few times

f) To have the trots

g) A camel toe

Don't fancy yours much
JE PRÉFÈRE DORMIR SUR LE CANAPÉ

To have fallen from the ugly tree and hit every branch on the way down
Etre moche comme un pou

This describes someone you wouldn't want to meet on a blind date. The origin of the English version is unknown, but dates from very recently. The idea is not only that you are the fruit of the 'ugly' tree and thus unappealing, but that in falling from the tree you were further touched by 'ugliness' by each branch you made contact with before hitting the ground. Ouch! The French expression is much older, dating from the end of the 18th century, and refers to the generally accepted lack of aesthetic qualities of the louse ('pou'). Why the louse when many other insects are equally, if not more ugly? Perhaps this has more to do with the perceived anti-social behaviour of the louse in spreading diseases: not only is it ugly, but it is also best kept at a safe distance!

To have a face like a bag of spanners
Avoir une tête de guenon
(To have the head of a female monkey)

To have a face like a bulldog chewing a wasp
Avoir une tête de crapaud *(To have a toad's head)*

To have a face for radio Avoir un physique de radio

To look like the back end of a bus Etre un thon *(To be a tuna)*

A swamp donkey Un boudin *(A blood sausage)*

A filthy pig Sale comme un peigne *(As dirty as a comb)*

To have a body like a badly packed kitbag
Etre un pot à tabac *(To be a tobacco jar)*

To be as bald as a coot
Avoir un crâne d'œuf

The greatest fear of the middle-aged man? This expression, meaning to have a receding hairline or, worse, be completely hairless, has existed in its English version since the early 15th century. The coot is a water bird, also known as the bald coot, which has the unfortunate appearance of being in the process of losing (or having lost) its hair. The French are less equivocal: if you have a skull like an egg, then your hair has not just receded, it has gone! You are an egghead, and not in a good sense.

Body for Baywatch, face for Crimewatch
Beau cul, sale gueule *(Lovely arse, nasty mug)*

As flat as an ironing board
Plate comme une limande *(As flat as a dab)*

To be just skin and bones N'avoir que la peau sur les os

As thin as a rake Maigre comme un clou *(As thin as a nail)*

A salad dodger Un gros plein de soupe *(A fat person full of soup)*

Body beautiful
LA NATURE FAIT BIEN LES CHOSES

**Drop-dead gorgeous
Beau comme un camion**

At first, this expression suggests an odd French aesthetic, since lorries are generally not deemed to be handsome or beautiful. In fact, it is most likely ironic in origin and has, over the course of the 20th century, come to mean good-looking. Not to be confused with looking 'like the back end of a bus', which is to be very unattractive. The English equivalent is clear: the person concerned is so good-looking, you swoon and fall to the floor, possibly already dead from your heart racing so fast.

**Not many of those to the pound
Il y a du monde au balcon**

In other words, the lady in question has an ample bosom or large boobs. It's usually said by a man, arguably himself a big booby. For those not used to the imperial system of weights, this might be confusing and is best explained in the context of a greengrocer's shop. If you were to compare the number of individual fruits in a pound of grapes with the number in a pound of large juicy melons, you would get considerably more grapes than melons for the same weight. The same would be true of larger mammaries. Here is an example of where the introduction of the metric system falls down: 'not many of those to just under a half-kilo' doesn't have the same ring. Be careful if making a comment about the capacity seating at the theatre or opera in France, since to say, 'There are many people on the balcony' could be offensive to any lady with large embonpoint close by. The origin is uncertain; it possibly refers back to the 'balconnet' style of bra, or just indicates that there is a lot of something present. The German 'There is wood in front of the hut' has a similar sense.

She's hot Elle a du chien *(She has some dog)*

She's got shepherds on the mountaintop
Elle a les seins qui pointent *(She has breasts which are pointing out, i.e. her nipples are protruding)*

To have a six-pack
Avoir des tablettes de chocolat *(To have slabs of chocolate)*

Hung like a horse (donkey) Monté comme un cheval (âne)

As strong as an ox Fort comme un turc *(As strong as a Turk)*

Built like a brick shithouse
Une armoire à glace *(A wardrobe with a mirror)*

Dressed to kill?
EN CHASSE?

She's wearing a pussy pelmet (!)
Elle a une jupe à ras de la touffe

That skirt is just a greyhound!
C'est une jupe à ras de la foufoune !

Her skirt is incredibly short. The French expressions refer to a garment which is at the level of either the tuft/clump of hairs, in the first version, or the front bottom (to be polite!), in the second. The second English phrase is a play on words in the sense that a racing greyhound is never far from the hare, or in this case 'hair'. Moving on quickly. The first English version refers to a style of hanging curtains: a pelmet is a short ornamental drape which conceals the curtain rail. In any of these cases, the girl in question is a brave lass indeed, especially if she has gone commando for the occasion!

She has a landing strip
Elle a un ticket de métro

A very modern expression which refers to hair removal by a waxing of the bikini area of long-suffering women. In vogue since the late 1980s hair 'styling' down below has many different shapes and forms from the relatively hirsute (American wax) to the ascetic hair-free (full Brazilian). Interestingly, the form which leaves a long thin strip of hair is known as a French wax and this particular 'model' is what our expression refers to. The English is easy to understand if you imagine how the landing strip on an airfield appears from the pilot's point of view. The French is less obvious, but anyone who has ever taken the subway or métro in Paris will know that the ticket to ride is characterised by a thin black strip on the reverse. Travelling on the underground may never be the same again…

Tramp stamp Tatouage dans le bas du dos d'une gagneuse
(*Tattoo on the lower back of a prostitute*)

Fuck-me shoes (!)
Des chaussures racoleuses
(*Prostitute's shoes / shoes for soliciting*)

To show your whale tail
Avoir le string qui dépasse (*To have your thong showing*)

To go commando
Ne pas mettre de sous-vêtement
(*Not to put on any underwear*)

A camel toe
Un pantalon moulant l'abricot (*Trousers moulding the apricot*)

A banana hammock Un moule bite (*A cock-mould*)

A budgie-smuggler
Un maillot de bain à poutre apparente!
(*Trunks with an exposed wooden beam*)

The collars and cuffs don't match
C'est une fausse blonde (*It's a fake blonde*)

He's flying low
Le petit oiseau va s'envoler

Watch out! This euphemism means he has forgotten to zip up his trousers and risks revealing his most precious bits to the world, and possibly being arrested for flashing. The English is probably a play on the 'fly' or trouser zipper, whereby to be 'flying low' means the zip has not been pulled up and safely closed. Although fly-front trousers were invented in the 17th century, the first recorded use of the term fly for the trouser fastening dates from the mid-19th. The origin of the French version is uncertain, but is possibly a play on two well-known expressions involving birds: 'L'oiseau s'est envolé', meaning what you are looking for has gone, known since 1432, and 'Le petit oiseau va sortir' ('Watch the birdie!'), used in photography from the late 19th century as a means of getting the subject to look at the camera and stay still while the photo was being taken. The 'petit' in reference to the bird is not, one presumes, a reference to the dimensions of what might be about to escape from an unbuttoned fly...

Young at heart
AVEC LE TEMPS

There's many a good tune played on an old fiddle
C'est dans les vieux pots qu'on fait les meilleures soupes

Or just because something/someone is old, it doesn't mean they are past their sell-by date. The French version even implies that something old (a pot or pan) might be better than something new. The expression refers back to the tradition in the Middle Ages of cooking in an iron pot suspended from the ceiling (see House-warming party, page 187). The pot would rarely be washed out; instead new ingredients would be added to the old tasty remains, creating a superior soup than if you had started from scratch. In French the expression is applied more frequently to ladies than to gents. The English version often refers to an old(er) man with a young female arm-candy, with the suggestion that his 'playing' days, whether the violin or the field, are far from over despite his advancing years. The sense is the same as 'There is life in the old dog yet' and dates from the early 20th century. To suggest the same idea, that age does not define capabilities, the Italians believe that an old hen makes good soup.

To be an old hand
Ne pas être une première main   (*To not be a first hand*)

To be a bit long in the tooth   Ne plus être de la première fraîcheur
(*To no longer have original freshness*)

To have been around the block a few times
Avoir roulé sa bosse   (*To have rolled your hump*)

To be getting on a bit
Etre sur le retour   (*To be on the way back*)

To have the shakes
Sucrer les fraises   (*To put sugar on the strawberries*)

You're only as old as you feel
On a l'âge de ses artères   (*You have the age of your arteries*)

A senior moment   Une bêtise de vieux   (*An oldie stupidity*)

Mutton dressed as lamb
Une vieille peau déguisée en ado
(*An old skin disguised as a teenager*)

To be no spring chicken!
Avoir de la bouteille

In other words, starting to get on in years or not as young as you used to be. A version of the English expression can be found in the early 18th century as 'now past a chicken', though the current phrase probably dates only from the start of the 20th. The idea is that the older the chicken, the less tender its flesh and so, on the dining table and in life, older birds might be seen as less desirable. The French version has a slightly happier connotation. The bottle referred to is a wine bottle, and the idea is that wine may be produced in barrels, but it becomes worth drinking only once it has had time to age in the bottle. In this sense, mature is not necessarily a pejorative, rather a valuable stage of development.

Bodily (mal)functions
LES PETITES IMPERFECTIONS DE LA NATURE

As deaf as a post
Sourd comme un pot
....

What? Pardon? To be hard of hearing renders comprehension in any language tricky. What is interesting is the way different languages describe deafness. The French are as deaf as a jug/jar/pot; the Germans as a stick/cane; the Italians as a bell and the Spanish as a wall. And we always thought that walls had ears…

To be cross-eyed
Avoir un œil qui dit merde à l'autre
....

It is tricky to know which eye to focus on when talking to someone thus afflicted. The English version is self-evident and less poetic than its Gallic partner. The word 'merde' is well known even to amateur French speakers and so one might be tempted to translate this expression as 'He has one eye which says shit to the other' – and well it might, since they are looking in opposite directions. However, there may be another interpretation. 'Dire merde à quelqu'un' means to wish someone good luck, as in the English theatre salutation, 'Break a leg'. So for the French, being 'squint-eyed' perhaps means to have one eye wishing the other good luck, presumably in trying to work out what to focus on, since they don't appear to work as a pair.

To have butterflies in your stomach
Avoir le trac
....

A wonderfully poetic English phrase to express the feeling of anxiety you often have prior to an important event. It is relatively recent, dating from 1908, at which time there was only one butterfly fluttering. This then became plural in the middle of the 20th century. The origin of the French expression is unknown, but it may derive from 'tracas', which means anguish or worry. It is slightly older than the English, dating from the middle of the 19th century, and is often used to mean 'stage fright', in the sense of nerves prior to performing in front of an audience. This nervous sensation is obviously not limited to the English or French nations. The Germans have 'limelight fever', while the Romanians have wasps in their throat at the thought of a live performance.

As blind as a bat
Myope comme une taupe *(As myopic as a mole)*

I've got a memory like a sieve Ma mémoire est une vraie passoire

To have bags under your eyes
Avoir des valises sous les yeux *(To have suitcases under your eyes)*

To have a bat in the cave Avoir un truc dans le nez
(To have something (i.e. a bogey) in your nose)

To turn your stomach Soulever le cœur *(To lift up the heart)*

To sweat like a pig
Transpirer comme un bœuf *(To sweat like an ox)*

To have a raging temperature
Avoir une fièvre de cheval *(To have a horse's fever)*

To be as right as rain
Se porter comme un charme *(To act like a charm)*

To have a frog in your throat
Avoir un chat dans la gorge

An unhappy pair of animals to find in anyone's body, since this means to be hoarse or have a sore throat due to an excess of phlegm or mucus. The metaphor somehow seems much more appealing. The frog here is not a Frenchman, thankfully; rather it's a reference to the croaking noise such pond dwellers make. When you are hoarse, your voice is croaky, so there must be a frog stuck in there making a noise. The expression is quite recent, dating from the late 19th century and coming from America. Any references to medieval medical practices of putting a frog in someone's throat to cure hoarseness are amusing, but probably fanciful. The French expression might have less to do with a cat and more to do with a play on words. While some might think it derives from the purring sound made by a cat or the poor animal's fur which tickles the throat, it is more likely to be a distortion of 'matou' (another word for cat) and 'maton'. The latter used to refer to the lumps found in curdled milk and came to mean anything which might block or obstruct. The association between lumps in sour milk and mucus blocking the throat is not too hard to make, and both are best avoided.

To see stars
Voir 36 chandelles
....

Star-gazing? Unfortunately, not for the person involved, since this expression means to have been knocked out or slightly concussed, usually as the result of a blow to the head. The French version has existed since the late 15th century, though at that time one saw only some candles, rather than a specific number of them. By the 17th century, in the writings of Paul Scarron, the concussed Frenchman saw 100,000 candles; by the 19th century the number had been reduced to the current 36. Either the blows had got softer or men tougher. Why 36? Unfortunately, the reason is unclear, but that number appears in several French expressions, such as 'tous les 36 du mois' (page 102). The English version is a little more prosaic and simply refers to the glinting gold lights you often see flitting in front of your eyes which can appear like a constellation. Interestingly, while both the Spanish and Greeks also refer to stars in their equivalent expressions, the Germans hear angels singing.

To black out
Tomber dans les pommes

This means to faint, or to fall unconscious for a short period when the blood supply to the brain is restricted. The English version is relatively simple to understand. When we lose consciousness, everything goes black, so our world can be said to be blacked out. The French is less obvious: unless they worked in an orchard or greengrocer's, why on earth should anyone fall in the apples when they fainted? There are two possible (connected) explanations for this expression, which appeared in the late 19th century. The first suggests that 'pommes' is a corruption of 'pâmes', from 'pâmoison', meaning to swoon. Undeniably, 19th-century women did a fair bit of swooning and this might seem reasonable were it not that 'pâmer' had not been used in spoken French since the 15th century. The second possible explanation refers to a letter written by George Sand (nom de plume of the 19th-century writer Amandine Dupin) in which she describes her state of exhaustion as being 'dans les pommes cuites'. 'Etre cuit' still means to be worn out in modern French, and perhaps it is the association of these cooked apples and the old word for to swoon that gave rise to the metaphor as it is used today.

To feel like death warmed up
Etre malade comme un chien   (*To be as sick as a dog*)

To be at death's door
Etre à l'article de la mort   (*To be at the article of death*)

To feel under the weather
Ne pas être dans son assiette

This expression, meaning to feel ill, sick or out of sorts, has an interesting French origin. Rather than referring to the lack of appetite that often accompanies an illness, the 'assiette' here is not a plate as in modern French, but a state of equilibrium. The root is the Latin 'assedere', to sit, and 'assiette' is still used to describe how an aeroplane flies or someone's position on a horse (like the English 'seat'). Thus to be not 'seated properly' means not to be on top form i.e. ill. As you might expect for a seafaring nation, the English version has a maritime origin. When sailors (or passengers) were suffering from sea sickness or other maladies, they were sent below decks to recover. Some believe this meant they were 'out of the weather', which then changed to the current expression. More probable is that the suffering seafarers ended up 'under the weather bow', ironically the part of the ship most exposed to rough weather conditions, which probably exacerbated any 'mal de mer' they were already struggling with.

Toilet humour
HUMOUR DE CHIOTTES

To spend a penny
Aller au petit coin

Among many other examples, these are euphemisms for needing to go to the lavatory. The English derives from the public loos in which you were required to insert a penny coin for admission to the stall in order to do your business. The price was still a penny in the 1970s, but on a recent attempt to enter a public loo in London this had risen to 20p, and can cost even more! The French expression, often used by children, probably relates to the fact that the toilet would not normally have centre stage in a room and you would be more likely to go discreetly to the 'little corner' in order to perform.

To go and see a man about a dog
Aller secouer Georgette

Another metaphor for doing your private business.

The English version is predominantly used by men, the French exclusively so. There are various possible sources for the English, as well as possible other meanings: to go and have sex with a woman, to buy illicit booze or to avoid answering an awkward question. In any case, it should probably be accepted as a good reason for someone excusing himself without asking anything more about the matter. The French version, 'to go and shake Georgette', seems particularly bizarre, not least because the 'thing' to be shaken at the end of the visit is overtly masculine! There are a number of alternative words for penis which are feminine in French, of which 'queue', 'bite' and 'verge' are examples. Jean-Christophe still sniggers whenever we drive past a sign in the UK which declares 'Soft Verges'. There also exists a diminutive of the 'queue' which is 'quéquette', and perhaps it was a small linguistic shift from this to Georgette and an even better euphemism. Certainly, Georgette doesn't seem to refer to any specific lady. Gentlemen, take note – you could also 'essorer le boa' (wring out the boa constrictor) or 'égoutter le poireau' (drain the leek) to achieve the same end.

The smallest room
Là où le roi va seul   (*There where the King goes on his own*)

To have a turtlehead (!)
Avoir la taupe qui bourre   (*To have a mole which fills up*)

A trouser-cough   Lâcher une perle   (*To release a pearl*)

To take a dump   Couler un bronze   (*To cast a bronze*) (!)

To have the trots   Avoir la courante   (*To have the runs*)

To poo your pants (!)   Chier dans son froc   (*To crap in your trousers*)

To talk to God on the big white telephone
Appeler Raoul

Some conversations are best not held...since both these euphemisms mean to be sick in a spectacular and noisy fashion. The wonderfully imaginative English phrase comes from Down Under (where else?) and is often invoked after a night on the tiles. For those for whom the image is not clear, the big white telephone is the toilet bowl and the words uttered are more accurately, 'Oh Goooooooodddd' as one vomits, or 'chunders' in the vernacular again. While the French might not have the same colonial influence, the expression is no less poetic. Poor 'Raoul' is invoked simply because his name has (vaguely) the same sound as the noise one makes while throwing up: 'Raaaooooouuuuullllll.' A charming, but informative insight into both cultures. What else did you expect from a section entitled 'Toilet humour'?

To be about to toss your cookies
Avoir le cœur au bord des lèvres
(*To have your heart on the edge of your lips*)

To park a tiger   Dégobiller   (*To unswallow, i.e. to vomit*)

A pavement pizza
Une gerbe   (*A spray – usually of flowers*)

To do a technicolour yawn
Dégueuler   (*To unmouth i.e. to vomit*)

His breath could stop a rhino!
Il a une haleine à faire vomir une famille de rats!
(*His breath would make a family of rats vomit*)

Leftovers
LES RESTES

To be like two peas in a pod
Se ressembler comme deux gouttes d'eau

Or in other words, to be identical. This can refer to people or objects and is often used about siblings who look alike. The French version, 'to be as alike as two drops of water', dates to the 16th century, though as far back as the 15th a similar expression ran 'as alike as two drops of milk'. The English 'like as two peas', dates from the same period, and it is a connoisseur indeed who can tell one shelled pea from another. For the Spanish, in their equivalent expression, it is difficult to tell one egg from another.

Don't judge a book by its cover
L'habit ne fait pas le moine

This expression, which advises us to look beyond the superficial to the worth within, exists in its French version in a number of European languages. This is probably explained by the Latin, *Cucullus non facit monachum* ('the cowl doesn't make the monk'), with the hood changing over time into the monk's habit. The Spanish have an identical phrase, while the Germans plump for the more secular and ironic 'clothes make the person'. The English version seems to be more recent, being found in print only from the start of the 20th century, and is easily understood. Just because a cover attracts you doesn't mean the book will be a good read...with the exception of this book, of course. Interestingly, another Latin phrase with a similar meaning is *Barba non facit philosophum* or 'the beard doesn't make the philosopher', despite what hirsute pseudo-intellectuals might have us believe.

He's got pins and needles in his leg
Il a des fourmis dans la jambe *(He has ants in his leg)*

To have a memory like an elephant
Avoir une mémoire d'éléphant

Head over heels Cul par-dessus tête *(Arse over head)*

Knee high to a grasshopper
Haut comme trois pommes *(As high as three apples)*

Ankle-biters Des petits morveux *(The little snotbags)*

As large as life En chair et en os *(In flesh and bone)*

It's as plain as the nose on your face
Cela se voit comme le nez au milieu de la figure

QUIZ ANSWERS

Don't forget to check the answers to the quiz.
See how many you got right...

1. Knee high to a grasshopper
2. To look like the back end of a bus
3. To have a face like a bulldog chewing a wasp
4. To have been around the block a few times
5. To have the trots
6. A camel toe
7. To do a technicolour yawn

a) Haut comme trois pommes
b) Etre un thon
c) Avoir une tête de crapaud
d) Avoir roulé sa bosse
e) Avoir la courante
f) Un pantalon moulant l'abricot
g) Dégueuler

EXPRESS YOURSELF
DONNE TON OPINION

J UST CAN'T FIND THE RIGHT PHRASE TO SUM UP EXACTLY
WHAT YOU WANT TO SAY IN FRENCH? The following should
help in most situations.

Try to match the French and English before reading the chapter to gauge your true level of expressiveness! Answers are at the end if you have run out of words...

1. Va te faire cuire un œuf !
2. Etre aux anges
3. Je ne le ferais pas pour tout l'or du monde
4. J'en mettrais ma main au feu
6. J'en ai ras les baskets
5. Il n'y a pas de quoi fouetter un chat

a) To be over the moon
b) It's no great shakes
c) I'd stake my life on it
d) Get stuffed!
f) I'm fed up to my back teeth
e) I wouldn't do it for all the tea in China

Oh yes!
ÇA BAIGNE

It's the dog's bollocks C'est de la balle	

It's the cat's pyjamas
C'est nickel chrome

It's the bee's knees
C'est le top

These expressions, which all describe something that is the very best, top notch, absolutely fantastic, have diverse origins. The English versions, which allude to cats and bees, derive from the 1920s, when it was fashionable to create a whole series of expressions coupling animals and a part of the body or clothing in order to express one's enthusiasm. Perhaps understandably, the 'cat's adenoids' did not last in posterity. Lumps on a different animal, however, did, and the 'dog's bollocks', while perhaps a little vulgar, is a modern play on the same theme. Why the canine's testicles should be so great is hard to imagine. From one ball to another and the French expression 'C'est de la balle!', literally 'It is some ball'. This is also very recent and is a form of slang. It is unclear what ball it refers to: various theories suggest that it refers to a bullet, something related to smoking cannabis or indeed another testicle.

I'll eat my hat
J'en mettrais ma tête sur le billot

This expression is used to convey a considerable amount of certainty in an outcome. The English version dates from the 18th century, though probably became more widespread after Dickens included it in *The Pickwick Papers* in the mid-19th century. The meaning is clear: I am so sure that something will happen that I will eat my hat if it doesn't. A rather extreme and unappetising prospect. The French expression is even less appealing. 'Billot' is the executioner's block, where one would be forced to place one's head in order for it to be cut off. Given the French reputation as enthusiastic guillotiners in the 18th century, one assumes that any French man or woman who would willingly place their head on the block must be wholly convinced about something. Vive Madame la Guillotine !

I was in stitches
Je me suis fendu la poire

The English version of this expression, which means I was laughing a lot or laughing very hard, dates back to Shakespeare's *Twelfth Night*, written in 1602. The English have clearly been able to laugh raucously for a long time, and there are a number of expressions which communicate this same idea of the sharp physical pain one has in the diaphragm when out of breath or exercising. Other such pleasurable yet painful expressions include 'to bust a gut', 'to split your sides' and 'to laugh your head off'. The sense of the latter phrase is incorporated in the French version. You might wonder why anyone would have spilt a pear when they laugh, but the 'poire' referred to here is another word for the face rather than the fruit. That makes much more sense. Other European nations have similar expressions for hearty guffaws: the Germans laugh a tree branch and the Italians laugh to split their skin, while the Romanians laugh with their mouths open up to their ears.

Full steam ahead!   En avant la musique !   (*Forwards the music*)

That's right up my street
C'est tout à fait dans mes cordes   (*That is completely in my ropes*)

I'd stake my life on it
J'en mettrais ma main au feu   (*I would put my hand in the fire for that*)

To be over the moon   Etre aux anges   (*To be with the angels*)

You could have knocked me down with a feather
J'en suis resté comme deux ronds de flan

In other words I was flabbergasted, very surprised, astonished. The date and origin of the English version are uncertain, but the idea is very simple. Normally, when standing, we humans have both feet firmly on the ground and thus are able to resist the forces of nature or gravity and stay upright. However, if we are completely taken aback by something, we become unbalanced, such that it would take only a prod from something as lightweight as a feather to make us fall over. The French expression is a little trickier to understand. 'Flan' is a type of wobbly custard, often served in a pastry case, which is why the word can sometimes mean 'quiche' in English. It can, however, also mean a type of coin dating from the Middle Ages ('flaon') or, more recently, a disc of metal from which coins are made. It can also mean buttocks, a different kind of wobbly substance, presumably with the sense that you would be so surprised by something as to fall backwards onto your rounded buttocks. Finally, in the 12th century, a 'flan' was a punch and so the expression could mean to be as taken aback as if you had received two punches. Choose whichever theory tickles you the most.

Whatever...
NI CHAUD NI FROID

It's nothing to write home about
Ça ne casse pas trois pattes à un canard

Aside from genetic mutations, it would be very unlikely to find a duck with three legs ('pattes'), which is why the French version of this expression to mean nothing special or out of the ordinary exists. Not only would you be very lucky to find a three-legged duck, but to break any or all of its legs would be exceptional. This is why not to do this is exactly the opposite, i.e. something banal. It dates from the early 20th century, but we don't know why or how the duck came to be chosen to represent the extraordinary. The English version's history is also uncertain. It is possible that it came from a military context, in which soldiers writing to their loved ones from battle had a restricted amount of notepaper or an allotted number of words to write and thus would select only the choicest memories or anecdotes to report back. Thus anything which wasn't of merit wasn't written about to those back home.

Without making a song and dance about it
Sans tambour ni trompette

Without making a great fuss, without making something seem more important than it is. A version of the French expression dates back to the 13th century and refers to military manoeuvres which, to keep them more discreet, even secret, would take place without the drum ('tambour') and trumpet ('trompette') accompaniment that usually heralded an army on the march or in retreat. The current French version dates from 1650. The English expression has uncertain origins, though clearly people have been overacting or dramatising events for a long time, even in England. Whether this derives from the old travelling minstrel singing about important or mythical events, or the music-hall singer who would have a whole song-and-dance routine planned out, is unknown. Perhaps the origins were too unimportant to remember...

To sit on the fence
Ne pas se mouiller   (*To not get wet*)

It's like water off a duck's back to him
Il n'en a rien à foutre
(*He doesn't give a damn about it*)

It's no great shakes
Il n'y a pas de quoi fouetter un chat
(*It's not enough to flog a cat*)

To be bored stiff   Se faire chier comme un rat mort (!)

That's not my cup of tea   Ça n'est pas ma tasse de thé

That's not cricket   C'est pas du jeu   (*It's not the game*)

That's a different ball game
C'est une autre chanson   (*It's a different song*)

No way!
HORS DE QUESTION !

Mind your own business!
Occupe-toi de tes oignons !

The sense of this expression, instructing someone not to meddle in your affairs, has been around as long as humans have lived in close proximity to each other. The English version probably derives from the 1st-century Roman philosopher Seneca's counsel, *Semper meum negotium ago* – 'I always mind my own business'. Wise words. During the 1930s a slang derivation, 'Mind your own beeswax', emerged, possibly originating in the colonial era, when women would sit by the fireside making wax candles. This idea of a women-only occupation is inherent in the French expression, which translates as 'Look after your own onions'. While the stereotypical Anglophone view of the French is that they parade about with a string of onions for sale around their necks, this isn't quite the whole truth. However, one possible theory for the French saying does involve real onions. A mark of female independence in parts of central France, apparently, was that women were allowed a small corner of the communal garden in which to grow onions; they could then sell them to earn a little extra money. It became common for their husbands to retort to any perceived female meddling in important masculine affairs, 'Oh, go and tend to your onions', and over time the phrase took on a more general meaning.

Get out of my face!
Lâche-moi la grappe !

In other words, stop bothering me and leave me alone. The English is easy to understand in the sense that someone is intruding too far into your personal space and needs to back off and stop annoying you. At least it is only the face in English, for the French(man), it is his 'bunch' (euphemism for testicles) which is under attack and needs to be released. Ow, or should that be Aïe!? The phrase also has a more refined form, 'lâcher les baskets' (let go of the trainers). This might seem odd to Anglophones, but it derives from another French expression 'coller aux baskets', which means that someone is literally glued to your trainers and thus following you around everywhere. How annoying!

Don't hold your breath
Compte dessus et bois de l'eau

In other words, don't bet or bank on something, since there is little or no chance of it happening. The English version is easily understood. Often we hold our breath in anticipation of something we expect to happen imminently. Since we can't live without oxygen indefinitely, at some point we would need to inhale, and would risk death if we continued to hold our breath in anticipation of something which may never happen. The French is ironic, since it actually has the sense of 'don't count on it' and dates from the 18th century as 'compte là dessus'. 'Compte (là-)dessus et bois de l'eau (fraîche)' is found from the 1820s onwards, though why one would count on it and drink (cold) water is unknown. It is possibly an amalgamation of another French expression 'vivre d'amour et d'eau fraîche', to live on love and cold water alone. Who can argue with that?

My arse!
Et mon cul c'est du poulet !

Or, to paraphrase, I do not totally agree with the statement you just made. For Americans, this could be 'My ass!' or even 'Bullshit!' The more polite Anglophone might say, 'My foot!' and the better educated French, 'Mon oeil !', but the meaning is the same. Why French disbelief should manifest itself by claiming that their bottoms are made of chicken is unclear, even to the French. The expression 'Mon cul !', which means the same thing, became popular as a result of Raymond Queneau's *Zazie dans le métro* (1959) and is often heard as an abbreviated form.

Get stuffed!
Va te faire cuire un œuf !
(*Go cook yourself an egg*)

You're getting on my wick
Tu me prends le chou
(*You take my cabbage*)

What's bugging him?
Quelle mouche le pique ?
(*What fly is biting him*)

Don't get your knickers in a twist
Ne te mets pas martel en tête
(*Don't put a hammer in your head*)

To drive someone round the bend
Faire tourner quelqu'un en bourrique
(*To turn someone into a donkey*)

To be fed up to the back teeth
En avoir ras les baskets
(*The trainers won't take any more*)

To have it up to here
En avoir sa claque
(*To have your slap*)

To be pissed off
Tourner son nez
(*To turn your nose*)

I would rather stick hot needles in my eyes
Je préférerais me couper un bras
(*I would rather cut my arm off*)

I would rather dig my eyes out with a spoon
J'aimerais mieux me faire pendre
(*I would rather be hanged*)

It's all double Dutch to me!
C'est du chinois pour moi !

...and so is absolutely incomprehensible. But why double Dutch? And why Chinese? The answer to the former lies in the rivalry between the two dominant seafaring, empire-building nations of the 17th century – the Dutch and the British. Long before they started to abuse the French, the British took the Dutch name in vain to describe anything shoddy, dodgy, underhand or downright unpleasant. Here one thinks of 'Dutch courage', meaning that you can't be brave unless you are also mildly inebriated. Thus, if something is 'double Dutch', the language is so inferior as to be mere gibberish, not only once but twice over. The French expression is less jingoistic in that you can replace 'chinois' with 'l'hébreu' (Hebrew) and even 'l'iroquois' (Iroquois, a Native American language). The Chinese and Hebrew examples date from the 16th century and are cited simply because their written form/alphabet is so different to the Latin alphabet used in French. Let alone hearing the language, the mere sight of those strange characters would be enough to make the average Frenchman of the era throw up his hands in despair. The reference to Iroquois is slightly more difficult, though since the 17th century the French Canadians have used the term in a perjorative sense and possibly it made its way into French-French as a result.

It's not worth jack shit
Ca ne vaut pas un pet de lapin
(*It's not worth a rabbit's fart*)

I wouldn't do it for all the tea in China
Je ne le ferais pas pour tout l'or du monde
(*I wouldn't do it for all the gold in the world*)

Save your breath
Pas la peine de gaspiller ta salive
(*Not worth wasting your saliva*)

I feel as rough as a badger's arse!
J'ai la tête dans le cul !
(*I have my head in my arse*)

Pull your finger out
Sors-toi les doigts du cul
(*Take your fingers out of your arse*)

If you can't stand the heat, get out of the kitchen
Si ça ne te va pas, prend tes cliques et tes claques
(*If you don't like it, take your things*)

That's below the belt
C'est un coup bas
(*It's a low blow*)

He's taking the piss!
Il charrie !
(*He carts*)

It never rains but it pours
Les ennuis n'arrivent jamais seuls
(*Problems never come on their own*)

QUIZ ANSWERS

*Don't forget to check the answers to the quiz.
See how many you got right ...*

1. Get stuffed!

2. To be over the moon

3. I wouldn't do it for all the tea in China

4. I'd stake my life on it

5. It's no great shakes

6. I'm fed up to my back teeth

a) Va te faire cuire un œuf !

b) Etre aux anges

c) Je ne le ferais pas pour tout l'or du monde

d) J'en mettrais ma main au feu

e) Il n'y a pas de quoi fouetter un chat

f) J'en ai ras les baskets

TIME FOR THE WEATHER
C'EST L'HEURE DE LA MÉTÉO

I T ISN'T JUST THE BRITISH WHO ARE OBSESSED WITH THE WEATHER. The French are equally interested by matters meteorological and temporal. The following expressions should help fill any conversation gaps, or serve as ice-breakers in any circumstances.

Try your hand at matching the phrases below but bear in mind that for the Gauls 'un temps d'anglais' does not mean a heatwave!

1. Pleuvoir des seaux
2. Dès potron-minet
3. Il tombe des oeufs de pigeons
4. Faire un vent à décorner les bœufs
5. Quand les poules auront des dents
6. Faire un temps d'anglais

a) To be Bank Holiday weather
b) And pigs might fly
c) To be blowing a hooley
d) There are hailstones like golfballs
e) To be bucketing down
f) At sparrow's fart

Singing in the rain?
CHANTER SOUS LA PLUIE ?

It's raining cats and dogs
Il pleut des cordes

It's raining stair rods
Il pleut des hallebardes

Perhaps of all the English expressions we discussed for this book, raining cats and dogs was the one which intrigued Jean-Christophe the most…particularly when the Anglophone couldn't actually give a definitive answer as to why it exists. There are a number of explanations ranging from dogs and cats living in thatched roofs and being washed out in a downpour to the more likely corpses of said animals drowned by heavy rainfall floating through the city streets as the sewers overflowed. The likely date is early 18th century, and one hopes the sewers have improved since. The French expression is more literal and refers to the size, shape and weight of the heavy raindrops which appear to fall like pieces of rope. (In Germany it merely rains pieces of string.) Stronger imagery is evoked in the subsequent expression. The 'hallebarde' or pike was used in war in the Middle Ages and the expression probably dates from around this time. Stair rods, thick metal strips used to hold carpets in place on stairs, describe a similarly heavy, possibly painful raindrop. Still, in the equivalent expression in Spain it rains toads and snakes, so for choice perhaps English and French rain might be preferable to that on the plain…

To be pissing it down
Pleuvoir comme une vache qui pisse (*To rain like a cow pissing*)

It's bucketing down Il pleut des seaux (*It's raining buckets*)

To be soaked to the skin
Etre trempé jusqu'aux os (*To be soaked to the bone*)

And the weather today is…
LA MÉTÉO DU JOUR

To be Bank Holiday weather
Faire un temps d'anglais

This might not be an 'official' expression, but anyone who has spent time on British soil will understand what it means. Typically Bank Holidays fall on Mondays, allowing workers to have a well-earned long weekend.

Also, typically, the weather will be beautiful the week before and after the day's holiday, but for the long weekend itself it will be ghastly. Torrential rain, howling winds, possibly even snow – and this for the Bank Holiday in August! As soon as one is back in the saddle on Tuesday morning, the sun comes out. For the French, the English weather needs no further explanation, since implicit in the phrase is wind, rain, fog and biting cold. In short, 'c'est 'orrible !'

It's brass monkey weather
Il fait un froid de gueux

....

It's colder than a witch's tit
Il fait un froid de canard

....

Brrrrr! In other words it is freezing cold. The first French version refers to the pitiful state of the homeless beggar. The word 'gueux' was known in the late 15th century and meant someone who was dependent on alms and forced to beg to scratch out a living. Often sleeping rough, even in wintertime, and with poor clothing and inadequate blankets, he or she would be the first to feel the icy cold temperatures. The second French expression refers to the practice of duck hunting which usually takes place in winter and involves sitting immobile for protracted periods waiting for the blessed 'canards' to appear. It was known by at least the 19th century. The second English idiom is modern and vulgar. Who knows why a sorceress' mammary gland should be chosen as an object of extreme cold: it is probably one of those things you should take as read! The first English expression has a number of possible sources. One explanation gives it a naval origin, with the 'monkey' being a brass tray used to hold cannonballs, which contracted in extreme cold. Another source suggests it refers to the brass monkeys (see/hear/say no evil) used as ornaments in the 19th century, from which it was a relatively simple progression to the weather being so cold as to freeze the tail or even the balls off the poor animal. Our expression avoids reference to any particular body part, to spare the monkey's blushes.

It's filthy weather
Il fait un temps de cochon   (*It is a pig's weather*)

It's scorching hot
Il fait une chaleur à crever   (*It's a heat to die in*)

To be blowing a hooley
Faire un vent à décorner les bœufs
(*A wind to blow the horns off the cattle*)

It's a real pea-souper   C'est un brouillard à couper au couteau
(*It's a fog to cut with a knife*)

I've got goose bumps   J'ai la chair de poule   (*I have chicken flesh*)

I'm freezing my arse off
Je me gèle les miches   (*I am freezing my buttocks*)

There are hailstones like golfballs
Il tombe des œufs de pigeons   (*Pigeon eggs are falling*)

The calm after the storm   Le calme après la tempête

Quick time!
RAPIDO !

Hold your horses!
Minute papillon !

In other words, hold on, wait, be patient, don't rush things. The English version comes from America and dates from the first half of the 19th century, when horsepower referred to four-legged creatures rather than the power of a motor engine. One would, literally, hold on to the horses' reins in order to restrain them, make them wait and prevent them from galloping off in a cloud of dust. There are a number of possible explanations of how the French expression came into being. One marries the concept of time ('minute') with the implied ephemeral life of a butterfly ('papillon'), suggesting that it is a good time to pause for reflection, given that the next stage of metamorphosis is death for the unfortunate insect. Another, from the start of the 20th century, suggests that if the butterfly moves too quickly between the flowers it is trying to pollinate it will be less effective and thus should slow down. Finally, and most probably apocryphal, is the notion from later on in the 20th century that an overworked waiter in a Parisian café was named Papillon. This drinking hole was often frequented by journalists/writers. Being heckled and beckoned from all quarters by his impatient clients, Papillon became famous for responding, 'Minute, minute, j'arrive !' His clients then took to teasing the poor waiter by themselves crying, 'Minute Papillon' before the poor chap had a chance to retort and the phrase gradually become more widely known.

To be a flash in the pan
N'être qu'un feu de paille   (*To only be a straw fire*)

Time and tide wait for no man
On n'arrête pas le temps qui passe   (*You can't stop time passing by*)

Before you could say, 'Jack Robinson'
Avant d'avoir pu dire « Ouf »   (*Before you could say 'phew'*)

It's water under the bridge
Il y a de l'eau qui a coulé sous les ponts

Rome wasn't built in a day   Rome ne s'est pas bâtie en un jour

---

A beastly time
BÊTE COMME LE TEMPS

I haven't seen him for donkeys' years
Je ne l'ai pas vu depuis des lustres

This expression, meaning I haven't seen him for a very long time, is actually a corruption in its English version. Irrespective of the fact that, according to *Brewer's Dictionary*, you never see an old donkey, the 'years' referred to are not temporal, but physical. In olden days, ears were often described as 'years', either by the less educated or as part of a rhyming slang. Donkeys' ears are very long indeed and so, eventually, the expression (using years) came to mean a long time. The French expression is equally confusing to the modern ear, since 'lustre' usually refers to a chandelier, as it does in English. But it also has a separate and unrelated meaning, which was more familiar in the 17th century: it was a period of five years. This stems from Roman times, when the Latin *lustrum* meant either a type of purging sacrifice which was required every five years, or a census carried out on a similar time frame. By making 'lustre' plural, the French expression designates an indeterminate but evidently long time of a multiple of five years.

At sparrow's fart
Dès potron-minet

...is very early indeed, at the break of dawn or, as a translation from another French phrase, 'à l'heure du laitier' ('at the hour of the milkman'). The English version dates from the start of the 20th century, though was known and recorded in Yorkshire dialect as early as the 1830s. It is slightly vulgar, but in an amusing way. Anatomy being what it is, one of the first things you might do in the morning on waking is to pass wind. Birds tend to wake up earlier than humans and so it is reasonable to assume that it would be the most common of birds, the sparrow, which would be the first to break wind at the start of the day. The French version also relates to bottoms. Originally, the phrase was 'potron-jacquet', where 'potron' derived from *posterio*, meaning posterior, and 'jacquet' was a squirrel. Thus the literal meaning of the phrase, from the 17th century onwards, was 'from the moment the squirrel's arse can be seen' i.e. as soon as the light improves and dawn breaks. By the 19th century, however, the squirrel had been replaced by the 'minet' or pussy cat, a well-known night prowler. Indeed, by 1862 the expression had become so well known that Victor Hugo named his street gang in *Les Misérables* 'Les Potron-Minettes', a reference to other nocturnal participants and activities.

Twilight
Entre chien et loup

We have included a comment on this expression simply because the French version is so evocative. Twilight, as per the OED, is the 'soft glowing light from the sky when the sun is below the horizon, especially in the evening'. It has long been regarded as an intermediate time, as well as being, in Scandinavian mythology, a period of decline and destruction, especially for those of a god-like disposition. The sense of being between two conditions is implicit in the French expression, which dates back to the 13th century, though it existed in Latin before then as *inter canem et lupum*. Twilight is thus when the light has deteriorated so much that you can no longer say with certainty if the animal you see is a dog or a wolf. If the latter, this lack of clarity of vision could well provoke a mortal destruction too!

As the crow flies
A vol d'oiseau   (*As the bird flies*)

In the dark all cats are grey   La nuit, tous les chats sont gris

---

One swallow does not a summer make
Une hirondelle ne fait pas le printemps

This expression, meaning that one instance of an event does not necessarily signify a trend, is a good example of how things change according to culture and geography. Reference to swallows and summers was originally made by Aristotle in the 4th century BC and the quote continues '...nor one fine day; similarly one day or brief time of happiness does not make a person entirely happy'. Who could argue with that? Well, apparently the French, since their expression, dating from the 12th century, refers to spring rather than summer. They are not alone in that – the equivalent Italian also chooses spring. The difference may be geographical, in that the birds flying back from their winter in Africa would pass over the south of France and Italy much earlier than they would reach the more northerly British soil. One other possible explanation relates to differences in translation. The Latin version of Aristotle's words is *una hirondo non facit ver*; ver exists even in modern times in the Italian primavera (spring), from which it is a small linguistic hop to printemps and an earlier sighting of the migratory bird(s).

Not on your life!
N'Y PENSEZ MÊME PAS !

Only in a month of Sundays
La semaine des quatre jeudis

If only indeed...but as this expression suggests in both versions, this is something that will never happen. For the British, as many other Christian cultures, Sunday is the day of rest on which one doesn't work, gamble, shoot or, in some stricter factions, wash the car. A month of days of leisure might be bliss indeed, even if, by the end of it, one wouldn't be able to see the road ahead to drive. The French expression is scholastic in origin and a version of this 'week of four Thursdays' existed in the 15th century. The reason is that Thursday was traditionally a day off for schoolchildren (now it is usually Wednesday). Hurrah! Interestingly, the original expression was a 'week of two Thursdays'; it had become a 'week of three Thursdays' by the 16th century and a 'week of four Thursdays' by the 19th. Now that is what you call inflation!

It's not got a snowball in hell's chance
C'est pas demain la veille   (*It's not tomorrow the day before*)

Once in a blue moon   Tous les 36 du mois   (*Every 36th of the month*)

Until the first of never
Aux calendes grecques

The English is self-evident; the French refers to the ancient Roman calendar, in which the first day of the month was called the 'calends'. It was also the day on which all outstanding debts were to be repaid. Since these days didn't exist in the Greek calendar, one presumes that the monies due were not repaid either…

And pigs might fly
Quand les poules auront des dents

A veritable farmyard of animals, but all with the same conclusion: never. Pigs don't have wings and can't fly and chickens don't have teeth and hopefully never will. References to English flying pigs can be found in the 18th century, by the end of which the French were referring to their toothy chickens, although the phrase did mutate in the late 19th century to 'quand les poules pisseront' (when chickens piss), before settling in its current form. It is difficult to work out why one animal should be chosen by one nation and another by another, particularly when, to boot, Spanish frogs will grow hair and Italian donkeys and German fish will fly in their equivalent expressions. We should hope that never means never, since that would be a scary European menagerie indeed!

To wait until the cows come home
Attendre jusqu'à la Saint Glinglin

...is to wait an incredibly long time, possibly for ever. Don't bother looking for Saint Glinglin in your saints' calendar, since he doesn't exist and so you will have a long wait until that day comes around. 'Glinglin' comes from the German 'klingen', meaning to ring a bell, and 'saint' in this context is a deformation of 'seing' (signal/ signature), which in Old French meant either the ringing of a bell or the bell itself. Often one would promise to pay someone on the 'Saint Glinglin', which for the less educated or less religious might be plausible, but in fact meant they were probably never going to see the money owed. The dual references to bells possibly relates to the perceived lack of intelligence in cows, who often wear bells, and thus emphasises the gullibility of the person being duped. The Rosbif cows may or may not be smart, but they are certainly not speedy, since the English expression refers to the leisurely pace cows adopt when returning from the pasture to the milking yard. It dates from the late 16th century, so the plodding beasts might just about have made it home by now.

QUIZ ANSWERS

Don't forget to check the answers to the quiz.
See how many you got right...

1. To be bucketing down
2. At sparrow's fart
3. There are hailstones like golfballs
4. To be blowing a hooley
5. And pigs might fly
6. To be Bank Holiday weather

a) Pleuvoir des seaux
b) Dès potron-minet
c) Il tombe des oeufs de pigeons
d) Faire un vent à décorner les bœufs
e) Quand les poules auront des dents
f) Faire un temps d'anglais

EASY LIFE
LA BELLE VIE

L IFE CAN BE TOUGH BUT IT IS ALWAYS BEST TO LOOK ON THE BRIGHT SIDE IF YOU CAN. How to express a positive approach to whatever life throws at you? How to say that metaphorically your glass is half full? More importantly, how on earth to express any of this in French?

Ease into matching the following expressions, then breeze through the rest of the chapter to the answers ...

1. C'est du gâteau
2. L'avenir appartient à ceux qui se lèvent tôt
3. Rire à ventre déboutonné
4. Finir en deux coups de cuillère à pot
5. On ne change pas une équipe qui gagne
6. Après la pluie le beau temps

a) To laugh your head off
b) If it ain't broke don't fix it
c) Every cloud has a silver lining
d) The early bird catches the worm
e) To be done in two shakes of a lamb's tail
f) It's a breeze

Easy peasy?
RELAX MAX

It's a piece of cake
Çela se fait les doigts dans le nez

This expression, meaning it's simple or easy to do, has an uncertain origin in its English version. It would seem to have come from America in the 19th century and is possibly a corruption of 'easy as pie', which refers to the ease of eating a pie rather than baking it! Historically cakes have had a positive significance, as in 'to take the cake' (or biscuit), and this association with an award or prize dates back to the Greeks. The French expression 'to do it with your fingers in your nose' is bizarre for the Anglophone, if not downright unhygienic or impolite. We all know that from a very early age children have an unpleasant habit of sticking one or more fingers in their noses, so clearly this is something that is innate and easy to do. However, the French phrase dates from the start of the 20th century and referred to a jockey whose lead in a particular race was so great that he could afford the time to drop the reins and stick his fingers in his nose, as a child might, and still win.

It's a walk in the park
Ce n'est pas la mer à boire (*It isn't the sea to drink*)

It's as easy as ABC
C'est simple comme bonjour (*It's as easy as hello*)

It's child's play
C'est l'enfance de l'art
(*It's the childhood of art*)

It's a cinch C'est du tout cuit (*It's all cooked*)

It's a breeze
C'est du gâteau (*It's some cake*)

It's as easy as winking
C'est bête comme chou (*It's as stupid as cabbage*)

It's crystal clear
C'est clair comme de l'eau de roche
(*It's as clear as rock water*)

It's no picnic
Ce n'est pas de la tarte (*It's not some tart*)

Actions speak louder than words
QUAND FAUT Y ALLER, FAUT Y ALLER

To pull out all the stops
Faire des pieds et des mains

To do your utmost, your very best to achieve something. The English version dates back to the mid-19th century and has a musical origin. The stops on an organ allow the organist to alter the volume of the instrument by regulating the flow of air to the pipes. When all the stops are pulled out, the volume is at its greatest and ear plugs are perhaps recommended. The Germans use the same metaphor. The French expression is more literal, since it implies using every limb possible to do what is required. This seems more logical than the Egyptian idea of working with your hands and teeth or the Dutch standing on one's head to express a similar notion.

Don't beat around the bush
Arrête de tourner autour du pot

In other words, get on with it! Do what you need to do! The English expression dates from the mid-15th century and has its origins in bird hunting, when one team would beat or thrash the bushes to scare the quarry out, while the other would wait with nets to capture them. A hunter who shoots the birds straight off with a weapon might not be more sporting, but he is at least more direct. The French version dates from the same époque and originally had the sense of someone who would sidle up, or around, the large cooking pot suspended from the ceiling of the dwelling in order to sneak some food without anyone noticing. Thus it was a means of doing something indirectly and only in the 19th century took on the secondary meaning of to hesitate or procrastinate. The pot referred to could be for culinary purposes or the equally functional 'pot de chambre' (chamber pot/potty).

To come clean
Vider son sac

This expression, which means to tell the truth or to make a full disclosure, possibly has its roots, in the English version, in religious practices. Part of the teaching of the Catholic Church is that by going to Confession and recounting all wrongdoings to a priest, you can be purged or cleansed of your sins. The first use of 'to come clean', however, is not found until the late 19th century, though the sense has existed in many older expressions such as 'to make a clean breast of it'. The French version, which dates from the 17th century, has two possible origins. The first relates to a secondary meaning of 'sac' as stomach, rather than simply a bag as it is in modern French. To 'empty your bag' in this sense meant, perhaps rather crudely, to defecate and thus to empty yourself of all content, whether it be words or digested food. Alternatively, the 'sac' referred to may have a legal connotation. Historically, lawyers would carry around legal files and documents in a type of roll or bag. During the process of a trial, the legal eagle would remove pertinent documents or pieces of evidence from his bag to present to the judge and jury, and so would slowly empty this bag to reveal the whole truth.

To be full of beans
Avoir la frite

This expression, which means to be in the pink of health, in good condition and bursting with energy, has an equine origin in the English version. Dating from the 19th century, it refers to the fact, known since Roman times, that if you feed a horse on beans he is going to be full of life and verve, prone to go like the clappers and possibly also full of wind. Riders and stable workers take note. The French expression also exists as 'avoir la patate', which dates from the start of the 20th century. 'Patate' is slang for potato, but can also mean your head. Clearly, someone who has a good or clear head is on sparkling form. Note that 'patate' is invoked in a number of expressions such as 'Il a une sacrée patate' or, roughly speaking, 'he has the devil of a head'. Modern trends prevail and potatoes began to be chopped up and eaten more commonly as chips (French fries?); thus by the 1970s the expression had also started to be known as 'to have the chip', as in our 'frite' version. Chopped, peeled or scrubbed, it means you are in splendid form!

To have other fish to fry
Avoir d'autres chats à fouetter

This expression, meaning to have other (presumably more important) things to do, has uncertain origins in both languages. Of the two, the English version is perhaps easier to understand. As an island nation England makes extensive use of fish in both its cuisine and its vernacular. There are few species that wouldn't be cooked and served at the dinner table, so it is logical enough that you might have other fish to fry or things to do. The French expression is slightly more perplexing, since whipping or beating cats seems a particularly odd and cruel métier for the citizens of any nation. The expression dates from the 17th century and, unhappily for our feline friends, cats and whipping appear in a number of expressions, not least 'Il n'y a pas de quoi fouetter un chat', used to indicate a trivial or benign task. In any case, French cats should be happy to live where they do; in Italy they skin their cats in an expression with the same meaning.

To call a spade a spade
Appeler un chat un chat

For an expression which means to call things by their proper name without euphemism or evasion, it is ironic that both the English and French expressions have come to exist via other words. The English spade was originally an ancient Greek tub, which was mistranslated by Dutch scholar Erasmus in the 16th century and has remained a spade ever since. The French 'chat' is a little more delicate. As in English, the 'colloquial feline' (dare we say pussy?) is often used in French to describe an intimate part of the female anatomy. Modern French uses the feminine (as well it might!) 'chatte', but as far back as the 17th century 'chat' was commonly recognised and the double entendre of the words often used for humorous purposes. The first recorded use of the expression as it exists today was by poet and satirist Nicolas Boileau in the mid-17th century. We suspect many French speakers are unaware of the slightly risqué origins of this seemingly innocuous expression…

🌴

To move heaven and earth Remuer ciel et terre

To follow orders to the letter
Obéir au doigt et à l'œil (*To obey the finger and eye*)

To turn over a new leaf Tourner la page (*To turn the page*)

To tone something down
Mettre de l'eau dans son vin (*To put some water in your wine*)

To take the plunge Se jeter à l'eau (*To jump into the water*)

The early bird catches the worm
L'avenir appartient à ceux qui se lèvent tôt
(*The future belongs to those who get up early*)

First come, first served Premier venu, premier servi

To hit the nail on the head Taper dans le mille (*To hit the thousand*)

To work like a charm
Marcher comme sur des roulettes (*To walk as on casters*)

To have more than one string to your bow
Avoir plus d'une corde à son arc

To take the bull by the horns Prendre le taureau par les cornes

To keep your ear to the ground
Garder l'oreille aux aguets (*To keep your ear on watch*)

🌴

An iron fist in a velvet glove
Une main de fer dans un gant de velours

This phrase, describing someone who exerts rigorous control or leadership, but conceals this behind a soft and gentle exterior, has a confusing etymology. The expression, identical in French and English, seems to have been attributed to or expropriated by Charles V (Holy Roman Emperor in the 16th century), Napoleon Bonaparte (18th–19th century) and one of the latter's former army commanders, Jean Bernadotte, who went on to become the oddly named Charles XIV John, King of Sweden. Bernadotte is said to have used the phrase in relation to the tactics required to rule and govern the French with any hope of success. It is possible that the root of the expression is significantly older, being based on the Latin *suaviter in modo, fortiter in re* (gently in manner, firmly in action), attributed to 16th-century Jesuit Claudio Acquaviva. Thus ends the history lesson. Interestingly, while the Italians also have velvet gloves, the Spanish glove is made of silk.

To show a clean pair of heels   Prendre la poudre d'escampette

A fault confessed is half redressed
Faute avouée est à moitié pardonnée

Two heads are better than one   De la discussion jaillit la lumière
(*From the discussion the light gushes out*)

To treat someone with kid gloves
Etre aux petits soins   (*To be at small care*)

Forewarned is forearmed
Un homme averti en vaut deux   (*A man warned is worth two*)

To eat humble pie
Faire amende honorable   (*To make honourable fine*)

Cards on the table   Cartes sur table

Half full, not half empty
AH ! ÇA IRA, ÇA IRA

To do something off the cuff
Faire quelque chose au pied levé

This means to do something spontaneously or unexpectedly. The English version dates from the early 20th century and originates in America. The idea behind it is that after-dinner speakers would often scribble last-minute notes or hints on the cuffs of their evening shirts as aide-memoires for their speeches. The French version is considerably older, dating from the 15th century, and its meaning is simple to understand. If you have decided, for example, to go to the loo, you lift your foot to make the first step. If your loved one then unexpectedly asks you to scratch their back, you are left standing, unprepared for the change in direction or activity, with your foot in the air.

To kill two birds with one stone
Faire d'une pierre deux coups

…is to achieve two things with only one effort. This is also known as a 'Scotch double' when applied to clay pigeon (or other) shooting, and in this form is a reference to the alleged stinginess of the Scots, since you need only one cartridge to take out two clays and thus save money. The expression, which is almost the same in French without explicit mention of birds, may well derive from Greek mythology and the tale of Daedalus and Icarus, his son. Kept captive by King Minos on the island of Crete, with no means of escape by land or sea, Daedalus attempted to take advantage of some of the birds circling high above their fortress in order to use their feathers to make wings to fly away. With the throw of one stone he managed to kill one bird and as the stone ricocheted killed a second. Other feathers which fell, but it is an interesting story at least. Other languages have similar expressions: the Germans and the Dutch kill two flies with the same swat, whereas the Italians take out two pigeons with the same broad bean.

A bird in the hand is worth two in the bush
Un tiens vaut mieux que deux tu l'auras

Wise words indeed, since it is surely better to have one sure thing than to try for two uncertainties and risk losing everything. A similar English version of this expression dates back to the 13th century, though at that time the unknown quantity was in the woods rather than the bush(es). It had taken on its current form by the late 16th century, but probably found wider dissemination after its inclusion in Bunyan's *The Pilgrim's Progress* of 1678. The French expression, first cited in the *Dictionnaire de l'Académie Française* of 1835, is more explicit. The 'tiens' is written with an 's', since this doesn't mean 'your' (i.e. le tien); rather is a conjugation of the verb 'tenir' (to have/hold) in the sense of 'to have in your grubby little paw'. Thus, something you have already in your hand is worth more than two things you will have or perhaps more realistically 'could have'. Or, as Mae West said in 1934, 'A man in the house is worth two in the street.' Who can disagree with that?

Finger in the air
A vue de nez

This expression, which means to estimate, guess or approximate something, reveals anatomical differences between the French and the English. The island dwellers, by necessity avid mariners, often needed to know from which direction the wind was blowing. The quickest and easiest way to find out is to wet your finger and hold it up in the air. Not very scientific, but relatively effective. The French expression derives from the idea of having a good nose for something, be it wine, perfume or sniffing something out. This Gallic idea of the nose combined with vision ('vue'), i.e. using at least two of our five senses, implies an altogether more accurate assessment than the simple English finger in the air.

You'll soon get the hang of it
Tu seras vite dans le bain (*You will soon be in the bath*)

To be done in two shakes of a lamb's tail
Finir en deux coups de cuillère à pot
(*To finish in two large spoonfuls*)

It doesn't do any harm Ça ne mange pas de pain
(That doesn't eat bread)

To have an ace up your sleeve
Avoir un atout dans la manche (*To have a trump in your sleeve*)

Every cloud has a silver lining
Après la pluie, le beau temps (*After the rain, the fine weather*)

If it ain't broke don't fix it On ne change pas une équipe qui gagne
(*You don't change a team which is winning*)

Let sleeping dogs lie
Il ne faut pas réveiller un chat qui dort (*Don't wake a sleeping cat*)

Don't look a gift horse in the mouth
A cheval donné on ne regarde pas les dents

The proof of the pudding is in the eating
C'est à l'usage qu'on jugera (*It's in using that one judges*)

To laugh one's head off Rire à ventre déboutonné
(*To laugh with your tummy unbuttoned*)

To throw caution to the wind
Faire fi de toute prudence (*To disregard all caution*)

In the country of the blind, the one-eyed man is king
Au royaume des aveugles les borgnes sont rois

Every dog has its day
A chacun son heure de gloire

This expression is more easily under-stood from the French: each person has their time in the sun or, more commonly in English, their moment of glory. Subscribers to Andy Warhol's philosophy might extend this moment to 15 minutes of fame. The English expression dates back to 1545, but probably found wider dissemination after it was included in Shakespeare's *Hamlet*: 'The cat will mew, and dog will have his day.' Lacking the same literary heritage, the French version merely says that each of us has our 'hour of glory', a moment of success or, as the Italians quaintly put it, 'our own ray of sunshine'.

It's in the bag L'affaire est dans le sac   (*The business is in the bag*)

A change is as good as a rest Changement d'herbage réjouit le veau
(*Changing the grass delights the calf*)

QUIZ ANSWERS

Don't forget to check the answers to the quiz.

1. It's a breeze	a) C'est du gâteau
2. The early bird catches the worm	b) L'avenir appartient à ceux qui se lèvent tôt
3. To laugh your head off	c) Rire à ventre déboutonné
4. To be done in two shakes of a lamb's tail	d) Finir en deux coups de cuillère à pot
5. If it ain't broke don't fix it	e) On ne change pas une équipe qui gagne

TOUGH LIFE

LA VIE NE FAIT PAS DE CADEAU

LIFE ISN'T PLAIN SAILING IN ANY LANGUAGE. Problems, lies, stress, anger and what is it all for in the end? Sadly, we don't have the answer to that, but in this chapter we can try to give you the phrases to express some of life's woes.

Tackle the obstacle of matching the following French and English expressions and, if you surmount the rest of the chapter, the answers are at the end. Good luck!

1. Mettre le loup dans la bergerie
2. C'est coton
3. Qui sème le vent récolte la tempête
4. Rouler quelqu'un dans la farine
5. Ecraser une mouche avec un gant de boxe
6. Faut pas pousser mémé dans les orties

a) Don't over-egg the pudding
b) It's a tough nut to crack
c) To pull a fast one on someone
d) To set the cat among the pigeons
e) Your chickens have come home to roost
f) To use a sledgehammer to crack a nut

Tricksters
BARATINEURS

An April fool
Un poisson d'Avril

The name given to someone who falls for a trick or practical joke on 1 April of each year. The English version is easy to understand – the person has been fooled and is thus a fool – and its first recorded use goes back to Chaucer in 1392. The French version is less obvious, and there are a number of explanations as to why it is an April fish in France (as it is also in Italy – one of the few other countries to play tricks on 1 April). Firstly, it could be a play on the word 'maquereau' or mackerel, which since the 15th century has meant a pimp or procurer. Not only is April a good month for mackerel fishing, but it is also the time when thoughts turn to courting and so the 'mackerel' may well have been a go-between who passed illicit love letters between amorous couples. We don't know why this implies practical jokes, unless the young mischief-maker deliberately mixed up love letters with untold consequences. Alternatively, it could be a reference to the impending end of Lent, during which meat was prohibited and even fish could only be eaten rarely. Why 1 April? The answer possibly lies with the Ancient Greeks, for whom the god of laughter was feted on a day which broadly equates in our modern Gregorian calendar to 1 April.

To make believe that the moon is made of green cheese
Faire passer des vessies pour des lanternes

...is to try to dupe someone into believing something or to 'pull the wool over their eyes'. The English version is on record as far back as John Heywood's 1546 *Dialogue of Proverbs*, though at this time it was written only that 'the moon is made of a greene cheese'. The addition of the 'make believe' came at a later, unknown date. The idea that the moon was made of cheese was widespread in folklore and fable, most commonly when a simpleton saw a reflection of the moon and believed it was a nice camembert. The green probably refers to the age of the cheese, i.e. an unripe brie still tends to have a circular shape like a full moon, though when it is more mature it starts running all over the plate and smelling to high heaven! The idea behind the French version, literally translated as 'to pass off bladders as lanterns', dates back to the 13th century. At the time pig bladders were commonly dried out and used for all manner of purposes – tobacco pouches and purses, to name but two. Since they were reasonably transparent, they were also occasionally used as lanterns in times of emergency, by means of a lighted candle being placed within the dried inflated bladder. Only the village idiot would have believed that such a haphazard lighting device involving the urinary tract of a pig could be a real lantern, and so the phrase came to exist.

To lie through your teeth
Mentir comme un arracheur de dents

...is to tell falsehoods without any shame, often in the knowledge that the person you are lying to knows you are lying! The English expression has uncertain origins and exists in a number of similar forms: you can lie in your teeth or lie in your throat as well as telling a bare-faced lie (since those without beards were mistakenly deemed to be more honest). The expression possibly derives from the fact that those who lie frequently smile while they do so, to give an extra sense of faux reassurance. This idea of false or shallow comfort is behind the French version, which dates from at least the 17th century in its current form. 'Un arracheur de dents' is a 'puller of teeth' i.e. a dentist, and the métier was known in this form from the 16th century onwards. At this time, dentists were glorified travelling torturers who frequented village fairs in order to solve the dental woes of the local peasants. Without effective anaesthetic, the cries of pain of the unfortunate patient having his tooth roughly extracted would be drowned out by the practitioner's sidekick banging a large drum, in order not to deter any other potential punters. One can well imagine why the phrase came into being. 'Is this going to hurt?' asked the anxious patient. 'Only a little bit' came the reply...cue drum-roll.

To tell pork pies
Raconter des salades

To spin a yarn, tell a tall tale or just to lie. The English version is Cockney rhyming slang for lies and is often abbreviated to 'porkies'. As well as being a pastry, a pork pie is a type of hat, popular since the late 19th century, and the expression may well have come from this 'titfer' (tit-for-tat or hat). Note that these pork pies are not to be confused with the Cockney 'mince pies', which means eyes. The French version is equally interesting, since why would anyone want to tell salads? The idea is that a salad is a composition of a number of ingredients which when put together have a nice taste and, more importantly, are easily swallowed, as good lies often are. Interestingly, in their equivalent expressions the Hungarians tell greens, while the Brazilians tell stories that send the oxen to sleep.

To pull a fast one on someone
Rouler quelqu'un dans la farine (*To roll someone in the flour*)

To take the bait
Mordre à l'hameçon (*To bite the hook*)

To swallow something hook, line and sinker
Avaler des couleuvres (*To swallow some grass snakes*)

An old wives' tale
Une recette de grand-mère (*A grandmother's recipe*)

To cover your tracks
Brouiller les pistes (*To blur the trail*)

To smell a rat
Il y a anguille sous roche (*There's an eel under the rock*)

As clear as mud
Clair comme de l'encre de chine (*As clear as Chinese ink*)

A blind spot Un angle mort (*A dead angle*)

To take something with a pinch of salt
Prendre quelque chose avec des pincettes
(*It's something to take with tweezers*)

To fudge the issue
Noyer le poisson
....

To cloud the facts, to tangle or confuse things so as to make them difficult to understand. The English version, which can also have a sense of to cobble together a solution or presentation in a rather underhand way, dates from the 17th century. Fudge probably derives from 'fadge', which at that time meant to fit or to be as expected; over the years it evolved to mean to fit together in a clumsy, perhaps dodgy way, especially when relating to facts and figures. The French expression, which dates from at least the 19th century, literally means to drown the fish. This might seem odd given that fish live in the water, but it refers to an old fisherman's practice. Once the fish had taken the bait/hook it was dunked up and down in the water in order to exhaust it as quickly as possible. Extending the metaphor, you exhaust the other person's ability to follow what you are saying because you hide the sense in a series of repetitive or complicated phrases in such a way that they eventually drown under a sea of words. Hopefully the length of that last sentence hasn't had the same effect on you! The Spanish have a similar expression which involves knocking out a partridge.

To laugh up your sleeve
Rire dans sa barbe
....

A rather unfriendly humour, since this expression means to laugh secretly at someone. The English version dates from the early 16th century and refers to the male fashion of garments with very full, puffy sleeves. These came in handy since you could easily cover or hide your face in order to make a joke at some unfortunate's expense. Originally the phrase was to laugh in your sleeve and only became up sometime in the 20th century. The French have a similar expression involving garments – 'rire sous cape' (to laugh under your cape) – but we have chosen 'to laugh in your beard' as it conjures up images of pantomime villains and theatrical props. The idea is the same:

you use the fullness of the beard to hide the fact you are smiling/laughing. This concept still exists in English in the use of 'beard' to refer to the fake 'girlfriend' of a (still in the closet) gay man.

Live with it!

LA VIE N'EST PAS UN LONG FLEUVE TRANQUILLE !

Give a dog a bad name and hang him
Celui qui veut noyer son chien l'accuse de la rage

The English version of this expression has two possible meanings: if you say bad things about someone they will stick, but also once you have a bad reputation for (doing) something it is impossible to shake it off. The hanging part is sometimes excluded, but the full expression was known by the early 19th century in its sense of being stuck (and thus hanged) with a bad reputation. The French version is closer to the first English one, spreading wicked stories in an attempt to defame someone. It translates as 'He who wants to drown his dog accuses him of having rabies'. Since no one would risk being near a rabid dog, we can assume that (social) death might closely follow. The original form, 'Qui bon chien veut tuer, la raige li met seure' (which is an Old French version of the same thing), dates from the 13th century.

To put your foot in it
Mettre les pieds dans le plat

To make a (verbal) mistake, a 'gaffe' or 'faux pas' (note the English use of words of French derivation here). The origins of the English version are moot, but it seems to date from the late 18th century. It is recorded in print in Brewer's *Dictionary of Phrase and Fable* (1894) as 'the bishop hath put his foot in it', though this referred to a general blunder rather than a verbal slip. The expression either came from or engendered the common phrase 'to put your foot in your mouth', which has the same meaning of saying something you really shouldn't. The French expression is slightly more recent, dating from the 19th century. At that time a 'plat' was an area of low water rather than its current meaning of a dish. Given its shallowness, anyone who put their feet in for a paddle would immediately stir up the mud at the bottom and mess up the clarity of the water.

To be hoist by your own petard
Etre pris à son propre piège

The French version is easy to understand: it is to be caught in your own trap, whether literally or metaphorically. But how on earth did the English version come to exist? The answer lies with Shakespeare, who coined the phrase for *Hamlet* in about 1603. At the time the petard was a recently invented explosive device used to blow up walls, buildings and the like. Sadly, 17th-century gunpowder was not reliable, so often the poor engineer who had set up the petard would also be blown up if the device went off too quickly. This is the sense of the hoist in the expression – to be thrust upwards, involuntarily in the engineer's case. The word 'petard' still exists in modern French and is used for small fireworks or crackers and also, for the more laidback, a spliff or joint. For the Italians, it is more likely to be a fisherman than an engineer who is trapped, since their expression runs 'to be caught in your own nets'.

A leopard cannot change his spots
Chassez le naturel, il revient au galop

The idea that what is innate cannot be changed is very old. Indeed, the English expression is found in the Bible, *Jeremiah*

13:23: 'Can the Ethiopian change his skin or the leopard his spots?' The French version is based on writings by Horace around 50 BC: *Naturam expellas furca, tamen usque recurret.* Quite. Effectively what Horace wrote, and what was put into its current form by the playwright Destouches in the early 18th century, is that if you try to change what comes naturally to you, it will come back in a much stronger form. A sobering thought.

To kick yourself S'en mordre les doigts (*To bite your fingers*)

You can take a horse to water but you can't make it drink
On ne saurait faire boire un âne qui n'a pas soif
(*You can't make a donkey drink if it isn't thirsty*)

You've made your bed, now you must lie in it
Comme on fait son lit, on se couche

Your chickens have come home to roost
Qui sème le vent récolte la tempête
(*Who sows the wind harvests the storm*)

You can take the girl out of Yorkshire, but you can't take
Yorkshire out of the girl
On peut emmener un âne à la Mecque, il n'en reviendra qu'un âne
(*You can take a donkey to Mecca, but it will still come back a donkey*)

You can't make an omelette without breaking eggs
On ne fait pas d'omelette sans casser d'œufs

It might seem obvious that to whip up an omelette you need what is inside the shells and so they need to be broken. Metaphorically, however, this expression refers to the fact that you can't achieve anything worthwhile without breaking or hurting someone/something; a sad truth often called 'collateral damage' in modern times. English sources attribute this to the French, possibly even to Robespierre, the mastermind of the French Revolution, and the expression was commonly known on British soil by the mid-19th century. French sources, intriguingly, make no mention of their infamous lawyer-cum-politician, though they agree that the expression in its current form came to be known during the 19th century. Interestingly, as far back as the 18th century, 'faire une omelette' meant to break fragile items and possibly the phrase developed from this.

Sticky situations
IL Y A UN OS

A fly in the ointment
Une couille dans le potage

A small problem or something undesirable which takes away the usefulness or attractiveness of an object. The English version comes from Bible, *Ecclesiastes 10:1*: 'Dead flies cause the ointment of the apothecary to send forth a stinking savour.' Definitely something to be avoided, as indeed is 'a testicle in your soup', as per the French version. The expression is slightly vulgar and is a modern and humorous take on 'un cheveu dans la soupe', a hair in the soup (see 'as welcome as a fart in a spacesuit', page 49). A bollock in one's Vichyssoise could definitely be seen as undesirable by the gourmet and to be avoided at all costs. On a less anatomical note, the Italians have a fly in the glass to communicate a similar idea.

Out of the frying pan into the fire
Tomber de Charybde en Scylla

The English version of this expression, which means to go from a bad situation to a worse one, dates back to at least the 17th century.

It almost certainly existed before this with various fish jumping from hot pans to hot coals, but its first recorded use in this form was by Roger L'Estrange in 1692. The French form has its roots in Ancient Greek mythology. Situated between Italy and Sicily, on opposite sides of the Strait of Messina, lived two dangerous creatures. Scylla was a multi-headed sea monster while Charybdis took the form of a whirlpool. To pass the strait safely, therefore, meant to negotiate either or both of these hazardous situations… and which was worse? *The Odyssey* recounts that Ulysses did make it, but only with the loss of a number of his crew. The expression came into common use in the 14th century and gained further recognition after being included in one of La Fontaine's fables in the 17th century.

To be left high and dry
Rester en carafe

In the English version this is another nautical idiom, meaning to be left stranded, abandoned or in a tricky situation. In its literal sense it refers to a ship which has been stranded on dry ground above the high-water mark, and as an idiom it dates from the early 19th century. The French version, from later in the same century, has a number of possible origins. The first suggests that in the slang of the time, 'carafe' was another word for the mouth – itself a receptacle for wine and water, among other things. 'Rester en carafe' was to be left with your mouth wide open, having forgotten what to do or say; over the course of time this took on the meaning of someone having been forgotten or abandoned. Another suggestion is that carafe was originally 'cruche', which usually means jug, but can also mean idiot or dope. Anyone who was forgotten by his fellow men on a desert island might indeed feel a bit of a twit and thus the expression came to exist. Alcoholics, note the difference between being left 'dry' in English and 'in the carafe' in French.

It's a tough nut to crack C'est coton (*It's cotton*)

To hit a snag Tomber sur un bec (*To fall on a beak*)

To put a spanner in the works
Mettre des bâtons dans les roues (*To put sticks in the wheels*)

To snowball Faire boule de neige

To be caught red-handed
Etre pris la main dans le sac
(*To be caught with your hand in the bag*)

In a pickle Dans le pétrin (*In the kneading-trough*)

Wide of the mark A côté de la plaque (*Next to the plate*)

When the shit hits the fan
Quand ça va nous péter à la gueule
(*When that will smash us in the face*)

You could hear a pin drop
On pourrait entendre les mouches voler
(*You could hear the flies flying*)

His jaw dropped
Il en a les bras qui tombent

In other words, he was dumb-struck, taken by surprise or left open-mouthed in response to a comment or a tricky situation. While the French can also be left open-mouthed ('rester bouche bée'), typically it is their arms that drop to express the equivalent level of astonishment. Why there should be this anatomical difference is anyone's guess, though the Germans react by having saliva taken away and the Dutch by having a suddenly broken clog.

Why bother?
POURQUOI S'EMMERDER ?

It's just like pissing in the wind
C'est comme pisser dans un violon

Both of which should be avoided, since the phrases describe a useless or futile activity. The English is relatively obvious: if you are trying to urinate into a prevailing wind, wet shoes, wet trousers and possibly even wet passers-by will ensue. The French expression is more curious. Why would you want to try to pee in a violin…especially when a double bass gives a greater surface area to aim at? Interestingly, up until the 19th century, 'pisser' was not considered vulgar and was the generally accepted word to urinate. As with its English equivalent, modern use is cruder; 'faire pipi' would be the socially acceptable form, even if it sounds a little childish to Anglophone ears. The French themselves are at a loss as to where this expression, first recorded in the 19th century, comes from. One possibility is that it is a corruption of 'souffler/siffler (blow/whistle) dans un violon'. In an orchestral sense, this might make sense: you can blow a trumpet or a flute to make music, but if you blow into a violin you get no notes and just look odd. Who knows? Perhaps the conclusion is that it is as futile to try to work it out as the activity itself…

Pearls before swine
De la confiture aux cochons

The English version, which refers to putting something of value in front of someone who is completely unappreciative, originates in the Bible, *Matthew 7:6*: 'Give not that which is holy unto the dogs, neither cast ye pearls before swine.' The French acknowledges the biblical reference, but instead of pearls, our curly-tailed farmyard friends are offered jam. Since pigs have a reputation for eating anything and everything, this is surely a waste of a luxury foodstuff. It isn't just the French who tempt pigs with sweet things: the Walloons offer them chocolate and the Spanish honey, while the Italians suggest that the same sweet nectar is not made for donkeys.

A fat lot of good that'll do me
Ça me fait une belle jambe

This expression, which means that something is of no help or use whatsoever, is ironic in both languages. The English is self-explanatory, the 'fat' qualifier serving only to emphasise the uselessness. The French version has a more historical background. It dates back to the 15th century, when it was fashionable for men to show their legs in breeches and hose. By the 17th century the curve of a man's leg was of paramount importance in high society and so the expression 'faire la belle jambe' (to do the beautiful leg – literally) was born. In the pre-plastic surgery and aerobics era, the shape of one's leg was determined by nature alone and so the expression started to take on its current ironic meaning – 'Cela ne me rendra pas la jambe mieux faite' (that won't give me better shaped legs), so what is the point in doing it? The current format has existed since the 19th century when, sartorially at least, men's legs were no longer a fashion statement.

To carry coals to Newcastle
Porter de l'eau à la rivière

This expression, meaning to do something pointless or superfluous, is more easily understood in its French version. Why indeed would you take water to the river, since there should be enough there already? The English is more interesting. Historically Newcastle (upon Tyne), in the northeast of England, was one of the country's leading coal-exporting ports and has been associated with coal mining since the Middle Ages. As such, the city had no need for any extra coal to be transported to it. It had more than enough already. The expression in its current form can be found as far back as Thomas Fuller's *The History of the Worthies of England*, written in 1661. For interest, the Germans take owls to Athens, presumably because Ancient Greece was the source of wisdom and the owl has long been recognised as the bird of sagacity in many languages, as in the expression 'as wise as an owl'.

Six of one and half a dozen of the other
Blanc bonnet, bonnet blanc *(White hat, hat white)*

A let-down   Une douche écossaise   *(A Scottish shower)*

Can't wait?
ÇA VOUS DÉMANGE ?

To be on tenterhooks
Etre sur des charbons ardents

To be incredibly anxious, strained or impatient about something. The English phrase in its current form dates from the mid-18th century and derives from the wool trade. Tenters were wooden frames which were used to stretch out freshly woven cloth and they were held in place by tenterhooks. The material would be stretched out for a period of time, thus giving the metaphorical sense of someone being both strained and impatient. The date of origin of the French, 'to be on hot coals', is unknown. The metaphor is clear, however: someone is so agitated that they are hopping from foot to foot in order to avoid being branded. The Germans and the Spanish use the same metaphor, whilst the Italians are on thorns to express the same emotion. Ouch.

To champ at the bit
Ronger son frein

One of a number of equine expressions in both languages, this means to be impatient or anxious to do something, often as a result of an unforeseen hold-up or delay. The French version dates back to the 14th century, where 'frein', or brake in modern French, actually meant the bit. For the less horsey among us, the 'bit' is the piece of metal placed between the horse's teeth, attached to its head by a bridle and controlled by the rider via the reins. Given the position of the bit, it is easy to see how a horse might chew at it if it has nothing else to do or is impatient to set off. This is the sense of the French 'ronger', which means to gnaw, and the English 'champ', to make a biting or chewing motion. The English version appears to have been recorded only in the early 19th century, though given the existence of the earlier French version, it is possible that the metaphor dates from much earlier.

To be like a caged lion Etre comme un lion en cage

To have itchy feet Avoir la bougeotte *(To have restlessness)*

To feel your hackles rising
Avoir la moutarde qui monte au nez
(To have mustard rising to your nose)

To blow your top Sortir de ses gonds *(To come off its hinges)*

Shit or get off the pot (!) Accouche ! *(Deliver/give birth)*

Any port in a storm Nécessité fait loi *(Necessity makes law)*

Don't jump the gun Il ne faut pas brûler les étapes
(Don't burn the stages)

To have a short fuse
Etre soupe au lait

The English version of this expression, which means to be quick to change moods or to have a quick temper, is easy to understand. Any explosive device with a short fuse will blow up more quickly than the same device with a longer fuse. In the same sense, someone with a thin skin will react to something much faster than someone with a thick skin. The French expression, which dates back to the mid-18th century, refers to the practice of heating up a soup made with milk, since the addition of the dairy product increases the risk that the whole pot might boil over more quickly than expected.

To fly off the handle
Prendre la mouche

This expression, which means to lose control, usually in anger, dates in its English version from the early 19th century and comes to us from the US. It finds its root in the ease with which a loose axe head can separate from the handle, especially when subjected to a hard blow. The French expression dates, probably, from the Middle Ages, when the word 'prendre', which today means 'to take', was used more in the sense of 'to suffer from'. At the time 'mouche' did not refer to the common housefly as it does today, but to all flying beasties which could sting. The phrase thus refers to the painful or energetic reaction someone might have after being stung or bitten. In addition, 'mouche' could mean worries or concerns; thus the expression meant to react to one's fears. For interest, the Italians steer clear of flies and axes and instead lose only their stirrups when they lose their tempers.

Don't count your chickens before they have hatched
Il ne faut pas vendre la peau de l'ours avant de l'avoir tué

This expression, which means not to take something as a given before it has happened, has very old origins in both languages. The

English version, which probably dates back to the 16th century, is logical to any farmer – until the chick has been born and is out of the egg, it is just an egg, nothing more. The French expression has a more literary basis. Its author is Jean de la Fontaine, famous 17th-century fable-teller, from whom many French expressions originate (e.g. 'la mouche du coche' or 'the gadfly'). Not selling the bearskin before you have killed the bear would seem equally logical to most people; however, for the two hunting friends in La Fontaine's tale, greed overcame common sense and while they were planning what to do with the money from the bearskin, the animal made his hasty escape to the safety of the forest.

We're not out of the woods yet
On n'est pas sorti de l'auberge

The English version of this expression, which means to be not yet out of danger or difficulty, is of uncertain origin. 'The woods' have traditionally been seen as a place of potentially nasty happenings, from Little Red Riding Hood to Hansel and Gretel, not to mention a group of teddy bears up to no good picnicking in the depths of the forest. The risk of remaining lost in the dark, confusing woods would thus lead to relief when at last the chink of daylight and the footpath back to safety could be found…if you were to be out of the woods, that is. At first sight, the French expression is harder to understand. Unless the 'auberge', or inn, is of a truly dreadful standard, why should it matter that you haven't managed to leave it yet? The answer lies in the 19th-century use of the word 'auberge' to mean prison or place of incarceration. An altogether different kind of 'gîte', and one which you would definitely be glad to leave!

Don't run before you can walk
Ne pète pas plus haut que ton cul

In other words, don't try to do something complicated until you have learned the basics. The sense of the English version can be found as far back as 1350, when we were reminded that the child crawled first and walked afterwards; however, by 1794, in a letter written by George Washington, this had become running before walking and has remained so ever since. The French version is on record from 1640 in Antoine Oudin's *Curiosités Françoises*. The idea of not farting higher than one's bottom is thus relatively old, if somewhat crude. A slightly more polite version is 'ne pas péter plus haut qu'on a le derrière', but the imagery is still the same. In similar idioms the Italians are advised not to make longer steps than their legs, and the Dutch not to attempt to jump a longer distance than their pole.

Going too far
DÉPASSER LES BORNES

To make a mountain out of a molehill
Se noyer dans un verre d'eau

Expressions for something of which more is made than is strictly necessary have been around since antiquity. The English version dates from the 16th century and perhaps explains why the Brits became such keen Alpinists given the relatively small size of the mountain to climb... The French instead attempt to drown themselves in a glass of water. Clearly, this is quite a tall order in any practical sense, hence the notion that you are exaggerating the scale of whatever problem you are facing. Interestingly, the vessel of French water has grown over time. In the 17th century one would drown in only a drop of water ('une goutte d'eau') or more unpleasantly in some spit ('un crachat'). In this sense, the glass of water seems a much better way to go!

He doesn't pull his punches
Il n'y va pas de main morte

This expression, which means not to hold back on something, has its origins in boxing in the English version. 'To pull your punches' is to deliver a softer blow, one which doesn't use the full force or weight of the body, often in order to let your opponent win. Someone who doesn't do this therefore gives their all, either in fisticuffs or metaphorically in words, actions or their criticism of others. The French version, which dates from the 17th century, has a similar pugilistic root. 'Une main morte' is one which is inactive, so if you were hit by it, you wouldn't feel any pain. By contrast, a hand that isn't dead could pack quite a punch, and this is the sense of the French expression. You are hit, verbally or physically, by a powerful hand.

That's a bit far-fetched   C'est un peu tiré par les cheveux
(It's a bit pulled by the hairs)

To use a sledgehammer to crack a nut
Ecraser une mouche avec un gant de boxe
(To crush a fly with a boxing glove)

He has his finger in more than one pie
Il court plusieurs lièvres à la fois
(He runs after several hares at the same time)

She doesn't do things by halves
Elle n'y va pas avec le dos de la cuillère
(She doesn't go there with the back of the spoon)

To run with the hare and hunt with the hounds
Ménager la chèvre et le chou

The English expression, which means to have it both ways, to try to do two apparently contradictory things at the same time, is an old hunting reference dating back to the 15th century. Normally one is either the prey, namely the hare, or the hunter, i.e. the hounds. To manage to be both at the same time is clever indeed. The idea of a problem to be solved is central to the French expression. It dates back even earlier, to the 13th century, in its original format 'savoir passer la chèvre et le chou' or 'to know how to get the nanny goat and the cabbage across'. This refers to an old logic problem: a peasant has a wolf, a nanny goat and a cabbage and needs to get them all across the river, but can only take one at a time in his boat in addition to himself. Which two should he leave behind without fear of one being eaten the other?

Don't teach your grandmother to suck eggs
Ce n'est pas à un vieux singe qu'on apprend à faire des grimaces
....

This has to be one of the strangest English expressions. The sense in both languages is to not to offer unwarranted advice to your experienced elders, who almost certainly know how to do it better than you anyway. Ah, the arrogance of youth. The English version dates from the early 18th century and refers, apparently, to the old tradition of pricking both ends of an egg with a pin in order to suck out the contents, which were then eaten raw or cooked. The intact shell could be painted or decorated, as was the custom at Easter. Perhaps this was common practice in days gone by, but it looks an odd pastime to the modern eye. The French expression is slightly less bizarre. Monkeys are well known for their ability to pull faces ('grimacer'), either as a form of communication between themselves or as mimicry of human expressions. Since Homo sapiens is not so far removed evolutionarily speaking from the ape, it is not for us to teach them how to stick out their tongues, though in this case the monkeys may well be justified in doing so!

To burn the candle at both ends
Brûler la chandelle par les deux bouts

Don't bite off more than you can chew   Qui trop embrasse, mal étreint
(He who embraces too much, has a bad grip)

Too many cooks spoil the broth
Trop de cuisiniers gâte la sauce   *(Too many cooks spoil the gravy)*

Don't over-egg the pudding
Faut pas pousser mémé dans les orties
(Don't push Granny into the nettles)

Making life more difficult than it needs to be
POURQUOI FAIRE SIMPLE QUAND ON PEUT FAIRE COMPLIQUÉ

To put the cart before the horse
Mettre la charrue avant les bœufs
....

Or to do things in the wrong order, often with a sense that they are back to front because they were done too quickly. Interestingly, the first recorded use of a similar phrase in the English language, in the 14th century, reversed not the cart and horse, but rather the oxen and their yoke and so was closer to the current French expression. This is presumably because it was a direct translation from an old French text. By the early 16th century, however – and it is difficult to discover why – the English phrase had changed to cart and horse and has remained so ever since. The French expression, putting the plough, 'charrue', before the oxen, 'bœufs', rather than the yoke of yore, dates from the 16th century. Clearly, this is the wrong way round, since how could the peasant expect his field to be ploughed if the equipment wasn't in the right place? It may be that he had other equipment on his mind, since there is a suggestion that the expression also meant to make love. The 'bœufs' are the testicles and the 'charrue' the penis, in which context the order is (anatomically speaking) the right way round. This second possible interpretation is not well known, and in modern French, as in English, the phrase is generally used to express something which is not in the logical order.

To be caught between a rock and a hard place
Etre pris entre deux feux

To find oneself between two equally unappetising situations, to be caught in a dilemma without really having a choice between the two. Surprisingly, the English version dates only from the 1920s and comes from the US, where it referred to being bankrupt. The French version is older, dating from the 17th century, and the 'feux' referred to are not 'fires', as in hearth or bush fires, but rather 'armes à feu' (firearms). The sense is thus that one is caught between two lines of shooting fire. A number of other possible sources have been suggested, ranging from druids to the dangers of cooking between two gas fires, but these are less plausible.

To split hairs
Couper les cheveux en quatre

The preoccupation of the pedant, since this expression means to quibble or to make fine distinctions over small matters. At first glance the French version, 'to cut hairs into four', seems an easier task to complete. Back in the 17th century, however, the expression was 'fendre un cheveu en quatre' or 'to split (rather than cut) a hair into four parts', vertically. While the English version does not specify into how many pieces the hair should be split, the French implies that this should be done at least twice to arrive at four parts. To boot, this mind-numbing activity should be performed on more than one hair since 'cheveu' became the plural 'cheveux'. We despair! Another recent (and more vulgar) French expression which encapsulates the same notion is 'enculer les mouches'. This translates as 'to sodomise flies', about which the less said the better.

To turn your nose up at something
Faire la fine bouche à quelque chose

To think something isn't good enough for you. Both expressions are easily understood if you imagine a baby/toddler who doesn't want to eat the yummy carrot puree you are trying to feed them. Revolted at the smell, it will thrust its head (and thus nose) up and away and press its lips together to prevent any food going into its mouth. The French expression, which dates from the second half of the 15th century, was originally 'faire la petite bouche', or the 'small mouth'. It referred to someone who was fussy about what they ate, as opposed to someone with a 'grande bouche', who would stuff whatever was on the table into their wide-open mouths. Over time 'petite' became 'fine' and the expression evolved to mean turning down, often in a slightly affected manner, anything you don't like the look of, rather than just food.

To build castles in the air
Bâtir des châteaux en Espagne

The English version, dating from the late 16th century and meaning to daydream or indulge in a fanciful idea or project, exists in this form in many other languages, not least German, Spanish, Dutch and Italian. While the Poles build their castles on ice, the French build theirs in Spain. The expression first appeared in the 13th-century work *Le Roman de la Rose*. It was further explained by the 17th-century man of letters Etienne Pasquier, who suggested that to build castles in Spain at one time had been absolute folly, since the marauding Moors would simply attack, conquer and subsequently live in them, probably quite happy not to have had to build the castles themselves. The French do make similar reference to other castles, in Asia and Cairo for example, but these expressions are much less well known.

To set the cat among the pigeons
Mettre le loup dans la bergerie *(To put the wolf in the sheep barn)*

Like looking for a needle in a haystack
Autant chercher une aiguille dans une botte de foin

To nit-pick   Chercher la petite bête   *(To look for the little animal)*

To sail close to the wind   Etre sur le fil   *(To be on the wire)*

To rock the boat   Jouer les trouble-fêtes   *(To play the spoil-sport)*

To miss the boat
Louper le coche

This expression usually means to miss out on an opportunity, but can also mean to fail to grasp the essentials of something. The English version alludes to a timetable of a regular service, whereby if you arrive too late the boat will have sailed. Why do the French refer to a coach instead? In the 16th century a 'coche' was both a horse-drawn passenger vehicle which travelled by road, and also a large river boat, similar to a canal boat, which was pulled along by a team of horses and carried passengers as well as goods. The idea remains the same whether water or land-borne transport is involved. Timetables must be kept to; if you are tardy you will miss your scheduled service and figuratively possibly the chance of a lifetime! The French expression can be used with 'louper', 'manquer' or 'rater', which are all commonly used in the modern language for when you miss a train or aeroplane.

QUIZ ANSWERS

Don't forget to check the answers to the quiz.
See how many you got right...

1. To set the cat among the pigeons

2. It's a tough nut to crack

3. Your chickens have come home to roost

4. To pull a fast one on someone

5. To use a sledgehammer to crack a nut

6. Don't over-egg the pudding

a) Mettre le loup dans la bergerie

b) C'est coton

c) Qui sème le vent récolte la tempête

d) Rouler quelqu'un dans la farine

e) Ecraser une mouche avec un gant de boxe

f) Faut pas pousser mémé dans les orties

WINING AND DINING
BIENVENUE CHEZ LES EPICURIENS

FOOD AND DRINK ARE IMPORTANT THINGS IN LIFE FOR ANY BON VIVEUR, and thus it is vital to be able to communicate the right level of appetite or thirst in the French idioms. Equally important is to know how to say that you have overdone it on the food or the sauce.

As an amuse-bouche, try to match the following French and English expressions before tucking into the rest of the chapter.
The answers will be served at the end of the meal.

1. Avoir les crocs
2. Il vaut mieux l'avoir en photo qu'à table
3. Avoir les dents du fond qui baignent
4. Etre sobre comme un chameau
5. C'est à réveiller les morts !

6. Avoir la gueule de bois

a) To be full to bursting
b) That'll put hairs on your chest!

c) To have a stonking hangover

d) To have the munchies
e) He can eat you out of house and home

g) To be as sober as a judge

Is your mouth watering?
A LA BOUFFE

I'm so hungry I could eat a horse
J'ai une faim de loup
··

Watch out, any animals in the vicinity, since this expression means that the person is ravenous or starving hungry. The English version has uncertain origins and probably is a derivation of 'to eat like a horse' which approximates in meaning to to eat like a pig i.e. to consume large quantities in a noisy fashion. Clearly, horses are large animals, so if you felt capable of tackling the whole beast in one sitting, you must have a large empty cavity for a stomach. There may also be a sense of the value of a horse as a working animal, such that if you were considering eating it rather than having it work for you, you must be very hungry. Finally, and possibly a more modern interpretation, is that horse meat, at least in Anglophone countries, is rarely seen on the menu. Thus, to be so sharp-set that you would consider eating Black Beauty or Trigger is to feel a great hunger indeed. The French version, to have the appetite of a wolf, dates from the 19th century. The wolf is often depicted in fame and fable as a hungry beast, to the point of eating skinny old grandmothers when there is nothing else on offer, and the current phrase refers to the wolf's propensity to devour its victims. However, in the 17th century, the phrase was 'manger comme un loup' or 'to eat like a wolf', and referred to the manner of lupine eating rather than the quantity consumed.

To grab a quick bite
Manger sur le pouce

Literally fast food, since this expression means to eat quickly, possibly even on the hoof, as opposed to sitting down and having a proper meal. The English version communicates the need for speed in two ways. Firstly, 'grabbing' is something which is usually done in haste, particularly when what is being grabbed or snatched is a handbag. Secondly, the 'quick bite' possibly refers to the opposite of good table manners, or at least what we were taught as children: that you should chew your food a certain number of times before swallowing. This advice stemmed from the Great Depression, when food was scarce and the stomach could be 'fooled' into feeling fuller than it was. Certainly, a quick bite does not imply the 15, 30 or 50 times that some food gurus would have us believe we should chew. The French version, 'to dine on the thumb', dates from the beginning of the 19th century. It refers to the idea of peasants working in the fields, who would take their lunch of bread and cheese with them in order to minimise the time spent eating and thus maximise the number of hours devoted to paid work. Holding his bread in one hand and his knife in the other, the peasant would cut a chunk of bread, push it onto the wedge created between thumb and fingers of the bread hand and then lift this to the mouth to eat. Efficient eating in practice! The Dutch have a similar phrase which translates as 'to eat in the little fist'.

To have the munchies Avoir les crocs *(To have fangs)*

To be sharp-set
Crever la dalle *(To die the slab)*

To lick your chops S'en lécher les babines

To eat like a bird
Manger comme un moineau *(To eat like a sparrow)*

To eat like a pig Manger comme un porc

Over coffee
Entre la poire et le fromage

In other words, the right time to hold a conversation, serious or otherwise. The French expression dates back to medieval times and is somewhat curious to the modern ear. These days your average bon viveur is used to eating the cheese course first and finishing with the fruit as dessert. In olden days, however, fruit was eaten immediately after the haunches of venison and wild boar, with the pear regarded as an ideal food for refreshing the palate. The pear is very important in French culture and features in a number of expressions in this book. The stomach full, this was the time to move onto matters verbal for the medieval French citizen. The English meal has tended to be less codified and typically it is over a beverage that Anglophones hold important discourses. The only surprise is that it isn't a cup of tea. The reason for this might be historical, since the introduction of coffee and thus coffee houses to Britain in the 17th century created a new venue for gentlemen to conduct their business. The insurance business Lloyd's of London came into existence at one such coffee house, proving that coffee was as important in the history and development of the English as tea!

He can eat you out of house and home
Il vaut mieux l'avoir en photo qu'à table   (*It's better to have a photo of him than have him at your dining table*)

His eyes are bigger than his stomach
Il a les yeux plus gros que le ventre

To stuff your face   Se taper la cloche   (*To bang the bell*)

To be full to bursting
Avoir les dents du fond qui baignent   (*To have teeth which bathe*)

She can't cook to save her life!   Question bouffe, elle touche pas sa bille !
(*On the matter of food, she doesn't touch her marbles*)

Bacchanalia
LE RAYON DE BACCHUS

To wet your whistle
Se rincer la dalle
....

As one might want to do after a long day in the office: have a drink, preferably an alcoholic one. The English version dates back to at least the 15th century, when 'whistle' referred to the mouth or throat and thus imbibing something would lubricate or wet this part of the body in need. In modern French 'dalle' means slab/stone, but back in the 14th century it was borrowed from the Old Norse daela, which meant 'sink' or 'drainpipe' and by the 15th had come to mean 'throat' or 'windpipe'. The expression itself dates only to the 19th century, when another alternative for 'boire' (to drink) was 'se rincer le corridor' (to rinse the corridor) and thus the expression in its current form came to exist. Cheers! Santé !

To drink like a fish
Boire comme un trou

....

To be an old soak
Etre une véritable éponge

....

These expressions describe someone who drinks a lot of alcoholic beverages. The English may have a reputation for drinking, but it is unfair on our aquatic wildlife to tar them with the same brush. In fact, the first English version refers to the mouth movements of a fish in water, open-shut, open-shut, and suggests that one who is no stranger to the bottle engages in similar activity, but with alcohol rather than water. The metaphor has existed since the 17th century. The first French expression, to drink like a hole, dates from a similar époque and refers to how quickly a hole appears to absorb any water that is poured into it. The same is true for the 'éponge' or 'sponge' which soaks up any liquid in its vicinity, hence the second expressions in both languages.

As sober as a judge
Sobre comme un chameau (*As sober as a camel*)

Bacchus has drowned more men than Neptune
Le vin a noyé plus de gens que l'eau
(*Wine has drowned more people than water*)

To be able to hold your drink
Avoir une bonne descente (*To have a good descent*)

To down in one Faire cul sec (*To make dry arse*)

Three sheets to the wind
Plein comme un tonneau

As pissed as a fart
Plein comme une outre

As drunk as a lord
Plein comme un œuf

The end result of drinking too much booze. The French expression 'Je suis plein(e)' can cause much amusement and confusion among locals when used by Anglophones, who tend to treat it as a simple translation of 'I'm full', having eaten too much Boeuf Bourguignon. More commonly, on French soil, it means to be drunk. The idea of being as full as an egg dates back as far as the early 1800s, according to Lorédan Larchey's *Les excentricités du langage*, complied in 1865. Both this and the expression including a goat skin ('outre') imply that one is so brimful with liquor that there is no room for anything else. The expression involving a barrel ('tonneau') is sometimes exchanged for 'comme une barrique' (wine barrel) and alludes to the full state of a barrel of alcohol…before the old soak starts drinking it. The origins, or even sense of, to be as pissed as a fart are unknown and it is the most modern and vulgar of the three. We advise against saying it to the Queen. However, 'as drunk as a lord' is a good example of the nobility on the razzle and the class system in operation. During the 18th century, the cost of alcohol was prohibitively expensive for all but the aristocracy. With money and time on their hands, it was not uncommon for the nobles to go on an old-fashioned 'bender' after which they would be, literally, falling-down drunk. Any commoner who attempted a similar inebriation might be said to be 'as drunk as a lord'. The third English expression has naval origins and dates from the 19th century. 'Sheets' are the ropes used on a boat at sea to hold or trim the sails. If these are not held tight, the sails can flap about and make the boat roll around as much on the water as a drunkard pitches and yaws between his seat, the bar and hopefully home!

It's like gnat's piss   C'est du jus de chaussettes   (*It's some sock juice*)

That'll put hairs on your chest!
C'est à réveiller les morts !   (*That wakes up the dead*)

To drown your sorrows   Noyer son chagrin dans l'alcool

To be half cut   Etre entre deux vins   (*To be between two wines*)

To have had one too many
Avoir un verre dans le nez   (*To have a glass in your nose*)

He's no stranger to the bottle
Il ne fait pas que sucer les glaçons   (*He doesn't just suck the ice cubes*)

Lit up like a Christmas tree
Rond comme une queue de pelle   (*Round like the tail of a shovel*)

Shitfaced (!)   Pété comme un coing   (*To be as smashed as a quince*)

As drunk as a skunk   Soûl comme un polonais   (*To be as drunk as a Pole*)

One for the road   Un dernier pour la route   (*A last one for the road*)

To have a stonking hangover
Avoir la gueule de bois   (*To have a mouth of wood*)

QUIZ ANSWERS

Don't forget to check the answers to the quiz...

1. To have the munchies	a) Avoir les crocs
2. He can eat you out of house and home	b) Il vaut mieux l'avoir en photo qu'à table
3. To be full to bursting	c) Avoir les dents du fond qui baignent
4. As sober as a judge	d) Sobre comme un chameau
5. That'll put hairs on your chest!	e) C'est à réveiller les morts !
6. To have a stonking hangover	f) Avoir la gueule de bois

THE ROOT OF ALL EVIL
L'ARGENT NE FAIT PAS
LE BONHEUR

NOT SEX, MONEY! It doesn't make you happy and it has no smell, but in any language it is better to have some money than none at all. Enjoy the richness of the differences between the French and English languages and the wealth of expressions in this chapter.

The cheap seats can start by trying to match the following expressions, the loaded might make it to the end of the chapter and the answers...

1. Faire bouillir la marmite
2. Cracher au bassinet
3. J'ai plus un radis
4. Travailler pour des clopinettes
5. Il serait capable de vendre père et mère
6. Gagner son pain

a) To earn your bread and butter
b) I haven't got a bean
c) He would sell the shirt off his back
d) To bring home the bacon
e) To work for peanuts

f) To cough up

Empty pockets
RIEN DANS LE POCHES

So poor he doesn't even have a pot to piss in
Fauché comme les blés

As poor as church mice
Pauvres comme Job

A woeful condition to be in, since all these expressions mean that you have no money. The first English version refers to the medieval practice for the common man, pre-lavatories, of doing his business in a (chamber) pot whose contents were then thrown out of the window into the street below. Someone who was particularly poor didn't even have enough money to buy said pot. One hopes their aim was good...

The second English phrase makes reference to the fact that at times in the past clergymen and their families tended to live a very frugal lifestyle, verging on poverty. As such, there was often nothing left over at the end of the day, not even a crumb for the mice of the household. The first French expression is a clever play on words which dates from the 19th century. 'Faucher' (to reap) not only describes the devastated state of the wallet of someone who is destitute (one imagines it in tatters after the harvester has passed), but also since the 17th century can refer to stealing or pickpocketing. 'Les blés' (wheat) would naturally be reaped and thus are a comprehensible addition to the metaphor, but with the additional twist that 'blé' at this time was slang for money. The second French expression is a biblical reference to when Job (in the book that bears his name) is removed from God's protection and taunted by Satan by having his wealth, family and health taken away. It's all a devilish attempt to make Job curse God. This he doesn't do and in the end he ends up wealthier than before, but it is his earlier state of being bereft which is referred to here.

To live a hand-to-mouth existence
Tirer le diable par la queue

…is to scrape out a living, using up whatever resources are at hand without being able to save any for the future. The English version possibly dates back to the 16th century and refers to the sorry state of much of the population, who without proper homes, work or money were forced to vagabond and take charity or alms to feed themselves. The idea of the expression is that the poor peasant was so hungry that he would take any charity and consume it immediately (from hand to mouth), without thought for the future, which indeed could be worse than his dire poverty of today. The French version is first recorded in the 17th century. The idea of 'pulling the devil by his tail' has two possible sources. One anecdote recounts that a desperate man calls upon the devil to help him out of his poverty. Satan subsequently appears, but makes to leave without actually giving any aid. However, before he can vanish in a cloud of sulphur, our wretched hero grabs hold of his tail to try to force him into action. A second story tells of a duel between a poor man and the devil in which, presumably to avoid being gouged by horns and long sharp fingernails, the despondent human attempts to tackle Lucifer from behind, by pulling on his tail. Tails are also invoked in the Romanian equivalent, 'to pull the cat by its tail', whereas Spanish poverty is manifested by having only two candles remaining.

I haven't got a bean
J'ai plus un radis   (*I don't have a radish left*)

To be in the red
Etre dans le rouge

To have a hard knock life
Manger de la vache enragée   (*To eat some rabid cow*)

Charity begins at home
Charité bien ordonnée commence par soi-même
(*Well ordered charity starts with yourself*)

For next to nothing
Pour une bouchée de pain   (*For a mouthful of bread*)

That's daylight robbery
Ça coûte bonbon   (*That costs sweetie*)

To be up to your eyeballs in debt
Etre endetté jusqu'au cou   (*To be endebted up to the neck*)

Lend your money and lose a friend
Ami au prêter, ennemi au rendu
(*Friend at the loan, enemy at repayment*)

To scrape the bottom of the barrel
Gratter les fonds de tiroir

To get stuck with the last of the selection of something or to choose (by necessity) something of inferior quality. The English version has uncertain roots, but possibly dates back to the 19th century. The idea that you would have no choice but to attack the dregs left at the bottom of a wine or beer cask gives a clue as to how desperate you are. Apparently the concept of 'the bottom of the barrel' was known in Ancient Rome, and was applied by Cicero to the lowest element, the dregs perhaps, of society. The French version is possibly an evolution of 'racler les fonds de tiroir', which means to scrape together every last penny. Here 'fonds' is used in the sense of funds or money, but can also mean the bottom of something i.e. the bottoms (plural) of a number of drawers (tiroirs), and the expression exists as both singular and plural. 'Gratter' means to scratch and conveys the idea of desperately scrabbling at the base of a drawer to try to find anything of value, metaphorically or otherwise.

To cost an arm and a leg
Coûter les yeux de la tête

That costs a bleedin' fortune!
Ça coûte la peau des fesses !

Expensive indeed, if one is willing to sacrifice body parts to pay for something. Why the English should chose limbs over the French eyes is unclear, and in fact there is no convincing explanation as to why arms and legs are chosen at all. Some reports claim this harks back to the tradition of portrait painting where a close-up head and shoulders was one price, but to add either arms or both arms and legs would substantially increase the cost. It is a nice story, but probably just that. Evidence of the French 'costing the eyes in your head' is to be found among other storytellers, Balzac for example, of the 19th century. One man's eyes are another man's limbs, it would seem. The second French expression is much more recent, late 20th century, and is simply a modernisation of the earlier phrase. 'To cost the skin of your buttocks' implies the skin being flayed off in slices, and an impending need for a soft cushion. Equally, a Frenchman could lose skin from his bottom ('cul') or his balls ('couilles'), though these are more vulgar. The second English expression, while not directly relating to body parts ('bleedin' being a way of avoiding blasphemy), does refer to another old expression, 'to pay through the nose' for something. This dates back to the 17th century when anaemia was common and many poor sufferers would literally bleed through the nose, in any circumstance. In this expression, however, one would bleed money rather than blood itself.

Money doesn't grow on trees
L'argent ne se trouve pas sous le sabot d'un cheval

Ah, if only it did, since it would mean a ready and easily available supply of notes and coins, rather than the opposite implied in this expression. In both versions there is also a sense of having to work for something, rather than have it fall in your lap. The date and origin of the English saying are uncertain. Perhaps it derived from a time when many people did mostly live from the fruits of the trees and hedgerows, a source of wealth which was readily available, as opposed to hard cash, which wasn't. It might also originate in the story of *Pinocchio* by Carlo Collodi, written in the mid-19th century. The hapless wooden puppet is taken in by the wily Fox and Cat, who persuade him to plant some of his hoard of precious golden coins in the field so that a 'money tree' will grow. He does plant his gold, but needless to say, since money doesn't grow on trees, the next day it is gone. No prizes for guessing who took it. The French expression in its original 17th-century form was 'ne se trouve pas dans le pas d'un cheval', where 'le pas' refers to the hoofprint. The most common thing found in or alongside the hoof prints of a horse (or donkey) is dung or manure; something arguably less precious and certainly smellier – and we all know that 'money has no smell'. Over time the expression changed to 'under the hoof of a horse' and has remained so ever since. For interest, something difficult to find is a 'white fly' for the Italians or a 'white blackbird' for the Spanish in similar expressions.

To rob Peter to pay Paul
Déshabiller Pierre pour habiller Paul

This expression, which means to use one debt/pot of money to pay off another, is interesting since the two versions are almost identical. In French poor Pierre (the French equivalent of Peter) is being undressed in order to dress Paul, which may or may not be better than being robbed, as in the English version. There are a number of sources which claim the origin of the phrase, some saying that it was a defiant stance against Rome and Catholicism (St Peter's) to deprive them of money in order to pay for the upkeep of the Church of England (St Paul's). Given that the expression exists in other languages besides English this is unlikely. More probable is the close association the two saints have – there are many churches which bear both names, and indeed they share the same Solemnity or Feast Day on 29 June, so to steal from one to pay the other was nonsensical. Interestingly, a version of the French 'découvrir Pierre pour couvrir Paul' was recorded in England as far back as 1611, in *Cosgrave's Dictionarie of the French and English Tongues*, but it is not known when the (un) clothing was updated to the modern form. The French also have the expression 'déshabiller Paul pour habiller Jean', which implies a third leg to the transaction and opens a whole new can of worms!

Big spender
DISPENDIEUX

In for a penny, in for a pound
Lorsque le vin est tiré il faut le boire

Not to do things by halves but to carry them through to the end. The English was recorded as far back as the late 17th century, though possibly became more widely known from Charles Dickens' *The Old Curiosity Shop* of 1841. From a country famed for its viniculture, it is not surprising that the French have a metaphor including wine. 'Tirer' in this context means to 'remove from a container', which in the wine business means pouring a glass from the barrel to check the colour, sediment and perhaps the ageing process. While it is in your glass, it would be a shame not at least to taste the 'vin', and this is what is meant here. The French expression can also have a sense of 'you've made your bed, now you have to lie on it', depending on the circumstances. To continue our analogy, this would presumably refer to having to taste a glass of corked wine.

You can't have your cake and eat it
On ne peut pas avoir le beurre et l'argent du beurre

A most frustrating expression, since it means you cannot consume or spend something and still possess it afterwards. The French version dates from the late 19th century and makes reference to a would-be wily operator who would like not only to sell you a pat of butter in return for some cash, but also to keep hold of the butter in order to sell it a second time over. If only. The expression can be found in a number of similar forms, including 'vouloir le beurre et l'argent du beurre'. Amusingly, it also exists with the adjunct 'and the milkmaid's arse too' ('et le cul de la crémière'). Now that is just being greedy. The English version is significantly older, having been recorded in Heyward's *Dialogue of Proverbs* of 1546. The sense is obvious; either you eat the cake or you have it, you can't have it both ways. A number of similar expressions exist in other languages, not least the Corsican/Italian version of wanting the barrel (of wine/beer) full and the wife drunk!

To go through money like water
Etre un panier percé   (*To be a basket with holes*)

To cough up   Cracher au bassinet   (*To spit in the money bowl*)

To throw money down the drain
Jeter l'argent par les fenêtres   (*To throw money out of the windows*)

Stingy
PINGRE

He's tighter than a gnat's chuff
Il n'attache pas son chien avec des saucisses

An expression to describe the miser. To be tight in this context derives from the 19th century and probably refers to the tight grip the skinflint employs to hold his wallet shut and ensure he doesn't have to pay for anything. The English version is slightly crude, 'chuff' being another word for bottom. A gnat is a very small creature and all parts of its anatomy are thus also small. The rest can be left to the imagination! The French version is equally humorous, if more polite. It dates from the mid-19th century and, even for those who do not love man's best friend, it should be obvious that, if you tie up your dog with sausages, eventually it will eat its way through them. The dog will not only have got free, but you will be left short of a lead and will need to tie it up again. The penny-conscious (or one might say simply sensible) French dog-owner thus does not indulge in this unnecessary extravagance.

A freeloader   Un pique-assiette   (*A steal-plate*)

As tight-fisted as a Scotsman   Radin comme un écossais

Look after the pennies and the pounds will look after themselves
Les petits sous font les grands sous   (*Little pennies make large pennies*)

He would sell the shirt off his back
Il serait capable de vendre père et mère   (*He would be capable of selling his father and mother*)

To go Dutch   Payer chacun son écot   (*To each pay our share*)

He's always first out of the taxi and last to the bar
Il a des oursins au fond des poches

Another expression to describe someone who is reluctant to spend their money. The English version is modern and may not be known to everyone. It derives from City life and the fact that he is who last in the taxi usually ends up paying the fare, while he who is first to the bar is obliged to offer the first round. The penny-pincher reverses the order and thus keeps the pounds for his or her exclusive use. As for the French expression, anyone who has spent time in the Mediterranean will know that a close encounter with a prickly sea urchin ('oursin') is to be avoided.

This is particularly true when you step on one with the fleshy part of your foot. So someone with sea urchins in their pockets would avoid rummaging around for small change, since they risk spiking their fingers on one of these 'hérissons de mer' (sea hedgehogs). Much better to let someone else pay…

Funny Money
PAS VRAIMENT HONNÊTE

To do a moonlight flit
Déménager à la cloche de bois

…is to abscond or do a disappearing act, often with the sense of not having paid monies due first. The French version dates back to the middle of the 19th century in its original form 'déménager à la ficelle', or 'to move (house) by the string/twine', where the rope would serve as a means of shimmying down from a window to avoid detection by the concierge. At the same time the expression 'à la sonnette de bois' was also in use. The idea here was that a wooden doorbell would ring less loudly, if at all, than a metal one and thus be less likely to alert the landlord or lady to whom rent was owed. This doorbell changed over time to a much larger 'cloche' or bell, though the furtive nature of the escape remained the same. The English version dates back to the Middle Ages, or at least the word 'flit' does – it literally means to move house. Shady behaviour knows no national boundaries and the English were also known to run away without paying the bill, though in this case at night-time, hence by moonlight, when there would be fewer people around and one would be less easily detected.

To fob someone off
Payer en monnaie de singe   (*To pay in monkey money*)

To bounce a cheque
Faire un chèque en bois   (*To make a wooden cheque*)

To buy a pig in a poke
Acheter chat en poche   (*To buy a cat in a pocket*)

He that will steal a penny will steal a pound
Qui vole un œuf, vole un bœuf
(*Who would steal an egg, would steal an ox*)

To line your pockets
S'en mettre plein les poches   (*To fill your pockets*)

Ill gotten, ill spent   Bien mal acquis, ne profite jamais
(*A possession badly acquired can never be taken advantage of*)

Money matters
QUESTIONS PÉCUNIAIRES

To put something by for a rainy day
Garder une poire pour la soif

This means to save some money now in order to safeguard against any future times of need. The English version probably dates back to the 16th century, since a similar phrase can be found in the translation of an Italian play, *The Buggbears*, in 1565: 'Wold he haue me kepe nothing against a raynye day?' The concept was probably that you might harvest or work only when the sun was out. Since you would not be paid if it rained, and the rent would still be due, it would be prudent to have a small financial cushion.

The French version, 'to keep a pear for your thirst', dates back to the late 1500s and was first recorded in 1640 by Antoine Oudin in *Curiosités Françoises*. The pear, of course, is a very juicy fruit for a weary traveller on the road without water. Thus it would be wise not to eat it but keep it safe in case of need. The Spanish and the Dutch also invoke fruits, but apples rather than pears.

Per head Par tête de pipe (*By head of pipe*)

Don't put all your eggs in one basket
Il ne faut pas mettre tous ses œufs dans le même panier

Don't bite the hand that feeds you
Il ne faut pas cracher dans la soupe (*Don't spit in the soup*)

To pay on the nail Payer rubis sur l'ongle (*To pay ruby on the nail*)

To sweeten the pot
Mettre du beurre dans les épinards (*To put some butter in the spinach*)

To earn your bread and butter Gagner son pain (*To earn your bread*)

Loadsamoney!
PÉTÉ DE TUNES

To be born with a silver spoon in your mouth
Naître dans la soie

Maybe this should be 'in one's mouth', since the expression indicates that one is born into prosperous conditions. It first appeared in English in a 1712 translation of Cervantes' *Don Quixote*. Spoons at the time tended to be made of wood or perhaps pewter; only the richest of families could afford silver ones. Whether the reference is to those spoons the family already possessed or the tradition of godparents giving a silver spoon to the newly born charge is unclear. A literal translation of the English expression does also exist in French, but we have included an alternative, 'to be born in silk', for interest. The silk presumably refers to either the silk bedclothes or the silk nightdress of the mother. Whichever, it seems a most comfortable way to enter the world – much more agreeable than in Italy, where wealthy babies are born with their shirts already on. Must bring a tear to the eye of Italian mammas.

A nest egg
Un bas de laine
....

In any language, one would be happy to have some savings put aside for a future date. The English version dates back at least to the 17th century in its current usage and arises from the common practice of encouraging a hen to lay more eggs by placing a porcelain (i.e. fake) egg in her nest. The idea here is that by having one, you will be encouraged to have or save more, be it eggs or pennies. The French expression has a similar rural origin. The 'bas de chausse' or stocking, which became the modern French 'chaussette' (sock), was used by country folk in the 19th century as a safe place to store their pieces of gold. A wool (laine) stocking was invaluable as a piggy bank in that it was always on your person and thus safe from unsavoury tricksters, or banks.

A backhander
Un pot-de-vin
....

A bribe or a sum of money (illegally) paid. The English version dates only from the 20th century, though one imagines the practice has existed since men and money first met. It presumably refers to the fact that if you show only the back of the hand, prying eyes can't see what is concealed within the palm. Backhanders did exist in the 19th century, though at that time they were glasses of wine, poured out of turn with the bottle handled backwards. Even today in Italy, pouring wine in this way is considered impolite, and even bad luck, since this was the way a drink might have been surreptitiously poisoned in days gone by. Wine is also inherent in the French, which dates back to the 16th century and literally means 'a pot of wine'. At this time the term had the same meaning as the modern 'pourboire' or tip (literally 'in order to drink'), since in French society you had to pay for the privilege of drinking wine. There was no hint of illegal activity or subterfuge in the original expression. This evolved over time and certainly by the 19th century, as evidenced by Zola's *Germinal* (1885), the use of pot-de-vin as a bribe had become well established in word and deed.

To be rolling in it
Rouler sur l'or

... is to be incredibly wealthy. The French dates back to the 18th century, but was cited from at least the end of the previous century in Antoine Furetière's posthumous *Dictionnaire* in the longer form 'rouler sur l'or et sur l'argent'. In modern French 'rouler' is most commonly used to mean to drive (a car), especially denoting the speed you are travelling at, but in this expression the sense is closer to the English: physically rolling from side to side on piles of gold and silver, perhaps because you can't help touching it since you have so much. The English expression is abbreviated from 'He's rolling in money', and you can also 'wallow' in it if you feel so inclined. Other nations plump for different activities to express the same idea: the Germans swim in money, the Italians splash about in gold, while the Poles sleep on the same precious metal.

To hit the jackpot   Toucher le pactole   (*To touch the gold mine*)

The goose that lays golden eggs
La poule aux œufs d'or   (*The chicken with golden eggs*)

To bring home the bacon
Faire bouillir la marmite   (*To make the pot boil*)

To grease someone's palm
Graisser la patte de quelqu'un   (*To grease the leg of someone*)

To make a mint   Se faire un fric fou   (*To make mad money*)

To have the Midas touch
Se faire des couilles en or   (*To have golden bollocks*)

To be filthy rich   Etre plein aux as   (*To be full of aces*)

To live like a lord   Vivre la vie de château   (*To live the life of the castle*)

To push the boat out   Faire des folies   (*To make follies*)

All's well that ends well   Tout est bien qui finit bien

QUIZ ANSWERS

Don't forget to check the answers to the quiz.
See how many you got right...

1. To bring home the bacon
2. To cough up
3. I haven't got a bean
4. To work for peanuts
5. He would sell the shirt off his back
6. To earn your bread and butter

a) Faire bouillir la marmite
b) Cracher au bassinet
c) J'ai plus un radis
d) Travailler pour des clopinettes
e) Il serait capable de vendre père et mère
f) Gagner son pain

WORK IT!
AU BOULOT

L IVE TO WORK OR WORK TO LIVE? Whatever your philosophy in the work place, you need to avoid making linguistic faux-pas in the office if you want to get to the top. We can't promise to free you from being chained to your desk, but maybe we can help you avoid being ridiculed by your co-workers for a slip of the tongue in the 'other' language.

Clock in by matching the following expressions.
The answers can be found as you clock out...

1. Se sortir les tripes
2. Etre au taquet au travail
3. Reçevoir cinq sur cinq
4. Avoir du pain sur la planche
5. Tirer les marrons du feu
6. Les carottes sont cuites
7. Tenir quelqu'un au jus

a) The die is cast
b) To reap the benefits
c) To slog your guts out
d) To keep someone up to speed
e) To hear it loud and clear
f) To have a lot on your plate
g) To be snowed under at work

The Daily Drudge
LA ROUTINE QUOTIDIENNE

The rat race
Métro, boulot, dodo

The French expression is more explicit in outlining the monotonous routine of those who find themselves on the hamster wheel of working life. Roughly translating as 'tube, work, sleep', the interminable cycle of the commuter is encapsulated in just three words. 'Dodo' is ironic, since this is a children's word for sleep. The 'rat race' has implicit connotations of a frenetic, perhaps fruitless human existence. The choice of a rat suggests that one has no more freedom in activity or decision-making than an animal in a lab experiment, at the whim of greater forces. Both are relatively modern expressions, but overwork would seem to be a human misfortune, for as Socrates wrote nearly 2,500 years ago, 'Beware the barrenness of a busy life.'

Rush hour   Les heures de pointe   (*The peak hours*)

To be packed in like sardines
Etre serré comme des sardines

Same old, same old
Le train-train quotidien   (*The daily routine*)

To get back into the harness
Reprendre le collier   (*To retake the collar*)

To bring grist to the mill
Apporter de l'eau à son moulin   (*To bring water to his mill*)

Office politics
La politique de la maison   (*The politics of the house*)

A Herculean task   Un travail de Titan   (*A work of Titan*)

Like watching paint dry
Long comme un jour sans pain   (*Long like a day without bread*)

To get down to business
Aller au charbon

The French version of this expression dates from the 20th century and literally means 'to go to the coal'. The modern interpretation is to knuckle down and earn a living (often if doing a dirty job), but this wasn't always the case. Far from associations with coal mining, the phrase arose in the 1930s in the context of prostitution to describe those who had a respectable job, as opposed to those who worked in the world's oldest profession. Over time 'aller au charbon' evolved to differentiate between any underworld and above-board activities before taking on its current meaning in the 1980s. The English expression is self-evident in the context of any professional activity.

To work like a dog
Travailler comme un forçat (*To work like a convict*)

To be snowed under at work
Etre au taquet au travail (*To be on the edge at work*)

To be as busy as a bee
Déborder d'activité (*To overflow with activity*)

To slog your guts out
Se sortir les tripes (*To get out your innards*)

To have your nose close to the grindstone
Etre un bourreau de travail (*To be a work executioner*)

To have a lot on your plate
Avoir du pain sur la planche (*To have some bread on the board*)

To work for peanuts
Travailler pour des clopinettes (*To work for fag-ends*)

To moonlight Travailler au noir (*To work on the black*)

On the job Sur le tas (*On the heap*)

It's not rocket science
Pas besoin de sortir de Saint-Cyr (*It's not necessary to pass out from Saint-Cyr [the foremost French military academy]*)

Don't hang about
Y a pas à tortiller du cul (!) (*No need to wiggle your arse*)

Pronto! Dare-dare !

I've only got one pair of hands!
Je ne peux pas être à la fois au four et au moulin !

....

The pressures of the modern work ethic. Juggling skills aside, the English version implies that you simply don't have any limb free to execute the extra tasks required or, in a similar expression, 'cannot be in two places at once'. The French idiom, which dates from the start of the 17th century, specifies exactly which places these are: it refers back to the feudal law whereby peasants were obliged to pay a fee to their overlord in order to use his mill to grind their flour and his oven to bake their bread. Obviously, these tasks were done in order – grinding, then baking – and so it wasn't physically possible to be at the oven ('four') and the mill ('moulin') at the same time. Middle Ages work-time management in action.

There was just the proverbial one man and his dog
Il y avait trois pelés et un tondu dans la réunion

Standing room only? Hardly, since this expression means that there was virtually no one in attendance at the event in question. The English version possibly exists in opposition to 'every man and his dog', especially in the sense of an invitation extended to everyone…even pet animals. In the context of a business meeting, it is not a good sign, unless the dog is particularly attentive. The French expression dates from the end of the 18th century. A 'pelé' can translate as a skinhead, whereas a 'tondu' is someone with very shorn locks, but in Old French both of these were used to describe undesirable individuals. This might have been due to perceived infectious diseases they were suffering from such as 'pelade' (alopecia) which caused them to be less hirsute. In any case, there were only a handful of them, and one might have been glad for that. For interest, the Italians and Spanish invoke 'four cats' in their expressions with the same meaning.

Make hay while the sun shines!
Il faut battre le fer pendant qu'il est chaud !

This expression, which means to take advantage of a moment or situation to do something, has the sense of the Latin *carpe diem* or 'seize the day'. The English version was recorded in Heywood's *Dialogue of Proverbs* in the 16th century and derives from the idea that freshly cut grass would be left in the fields to dry before being gathered in as hay. If it rained before this happened, the hay would be spoilt, so it was best to exploit good weather for harvesting while it lasted. The French expression is significantly older, from the late 13th century, in its original form 'len doit batre le fer tandis cum il est chauz'. The same expression, 'to strike while the iron is hot' also exists in English, as it does in a multitude of other languages, possibly because the principles of the blacksmith's trade are the same the world over. When iron is hot it is much more malleable and easier to shape than a piece of cold metal. The English translation probably found a greater audience due to its inclusion in Chaucer's *Tale of Melibee* of 1382, but the expression had been known across the Channel throughout the 14th century, so it is possible that Chaucer 'borrowed' it from the French.

The way to the top?
LES CLÉS DU SUCCÈS

To know your onions
En connaître un rayon

Is to know your stuff, to be knowledgeable about something. The origins of the English version are uncertain, and was first recorded in the early 20th century. Horticulture aside, one theory suggests that Onions was in fact the name of a revered lexicographer and editor of the *Oxford English Dictionary*. A renowned polyglot, he certainly knew his stuff, and someone who could do the same could be said to 'know his onions'. Even if apocryphal, it is a nice story. The French expression dates from the mid 19th century and the development of the 'Grands Magasins', or department stores. These were, and still are, made up of different departments, 'rayon', each catering to specific products – haberdashery, kitchen products etc. Each 'rayon' would employ someone who had detailed knowledge of the specific products on sale in his or her department in order to best serve the customer. Over time the expression evolved from shopping to those who know a thing or two about life in general.

To have a good head for business
Avoir la bosse du commerce

...is to have a natural ability or special talent to do something. The English expression is also used for heights, figures, maths and its meaning is self-evident. The French version literally translates as 'to have the bump' for business, which seems nonsensical. However, in the 19th century the pseudo-science of phrenology was in fashion and many people believed that the shape of someone's skull could point to specific skills, aptitudes and/or criminal tendencies. Someone with a pronounced forehead was believed to have a 'good head' for maths or figures, hence they had the correct 'bosse'. We are unsure where the right bump for business might be situated...

To be worth your weight in gold
Valoir son pesant d'or

...makes you a valuable member of the team, especially if you are plus-size. This expression, meaning that someone is very useful or worthy, is based on the premise that gold is the most precious metal. Since it is normally assessed in ounces, weighing a human being in the same terms could create a huge monetary value. The expression has existed in French since the 13th century, though a modern ironic twist replaces 'd'or' with 'cacahuètes' (peanuts). Infinitely less valuable. Up until the 17th century you could also be worth your weight in lead, 'de plomb', another heavy but substantially less precious metal, but again this had more ironic overtones. Peanuts, lead or gold...you decide the value of your co-workers.

To know something like the back of your hand
Connaître quelque chose comme sa poche (*To know it like your pocket*)

Many hands make light work
A beaucoup d'ouvriers, la tâche est aisée
(*With lots of workers the task is easy*)

To earn your spurs   Gagner ses galons (*To earn your stripes*)

To reap the benefits
Tirer les marrons du feu (*To pull the chestnuts out of the fire*)

To have a cushy job
Avoir une bonne planque (*To have a good hideout*)

Practice makes perfect
C'est en forgeant qu'on devient forgeron (*It's by forging that one becomes a blacksmith*)

To be a smash hit
Faire un tabac

...is to be a great success, to be very well received. The French expression, which dates only from the 1970s, has nothing to do with tobacco, which is the most frequent meaning of 'tabac'. Instead, it probably derives from 'tabasser', meaning to beat, and in this sense implies the noise of two hands clapping, the appreciative stamping of feet or a tumultuous round of applause. Noise, this time of something breaking, is also implied in the English version. Why exactly something should smash in order to be a hit in English is unclear, unless it is so good that it blows away/up all expectations. As long as it makes a splash, who cares?

To sell like hot cakes
Se vendre comme des petits pains

Said of a product that sells very quickly, without your even trying and often in great quantity. Anyone who works on commission dreams of this! The English version is almost certainly 19th-century North American in origin and the cake in question would have been closer to the pancakes or flat scones that were often served at village fairs or 'fêtes'. Cooked in short time and dripping in pork fat, they were so good, in fact, that they almost sold themselves, hence the current phrase. At first glance, the French 19th-century expression using 'little breads' seems slightly healthier. In fact, 'comme des petits pains', meaning in great quantity, can be used with a number of verbs besides 'se vendre', including 's'enlever' (to remove/take off) and 'partir' (to leave), though the meaning is the same; if you don't 'get your skates on', there won't be any left!

To be going places
Petit à petit l'oiseau fait son nid   *(Little by little the bird makes its nest)*

A big cheese   Une grosse légume   *(A big vegetable)*

To be head and shoulders above the rest
Etre à cent coudées au-dessus des autres
(To be at a hundred cubits above the others)

To be in the boss's good books
Etre dans les petits papiers du chef

A good place to be, since both these expressions mean that you are liked by your boss and are in his favour. Roll on payday! The English version probably derives from an idiom with the opposite meaning: 'to be in someone's black or bad books'. Though 'one's books' has been known since the Middle Ages to mean one's standing or reputation, black books date from the 16th century as places where the names and misdemeanours of criminals were recorded. The French version in its current form dates from the 19th century, although a similar expression without the 'petit' was known a hundred years earlier. 'To be in the papers' of someone meant being worthy of mention in either correspondence or private diaries, but only in a positive sense. The addition of 'petit' conjures the image of a rolodex or card index of positive information kept on a person. Employees be warned!

A brown-noser Un lèche-cul *(An arse-licker)*

To bow and scrape
Faire des ronds de jambe *(To make circles with your leg)*

To be the boss's blue-eyed boy
Etre la coqueluche du chef *(To be the idol of the boss)*

To give a leg up to someone
Faire la courte échelle à quelqu'un
(To make a short ladder for someone)

To be hand-picked Etre trié sur le volet *(To be sorted on the shutter)*

A stab in the back
Un coup de Jarnac

This English expression, which means a betrayal or doing something secretly to harm another person, probably refers to Julius Caesar's assassination in 44 BC. Whether the phrase comes from the event itself or from Shakespeare's play is unknown, though given the playwright's influence on the English language the latter is a distinct possibility. Caesar died from 23 stab wounds, one of which was inflicted by his trusted friend Brutus, who reputedly stabbed him in the back as Caesar tried to defend himself. The French expression is based on a duel in the 16th century between two noblemen, one of whom was the Baron de Jarnac. The Baron was accused of writing letters implying scurrilous behaviour by the then king, Henri II. Despite the fact that his opponent, La Châtaigneraie, a favourite of His Majesty, was the superior swordsman, Jarnac managed to stab him in the back of his knee – an unusual, but not illegal blow from which the Royalist bled to death. Although the strike may have been unethical, the witnesses could not deem it impermissible and thereby exonerate the king. In the 18th century, Jesuit revisionists re-evaluated the duel as treason, or at least a betrayal, and the term has remained in use in this sense ever since.

To stick to the script Rester dans les clous *(To stay in the nails)*

To keep someone up to speed
Tenir quelqu'un au jus *(To keep someone in the juice)*

To hear it loud and clear
Recevoir cinq sur cinq *(To receive five out of five)*

An empty promise Une promesse de Gascon *(A Gascony promise)*

To worm something out of someone Tirer les vers du nez à quelqu'un
(To pull the worms out of someone's nose)

Under someone's thumb
Sous la coupe de quelqu'un *(Under the cut of someone)*

When the cat's away the mice will play
Quand le chat n'est pas là, les souris dansent
(When the cat isn't there the mice dance)

To be power-hungry Avoir les dents qui raient le parquet
(To have teeth that scratch the wooden floor)

Management skills

LES PETITS CHEFS

The Kingpin
Le Grand Manitou

The big boss, the head honcho and possibly someone to suck up to in the office if you want to be promoted. The French expression dates from the early 19th century, though 'manitou' had first appeared in French usage some 200 years previously. It is an Algonquian (Native American) word for a spirit being, with the Gitche Manitou being a supreme spirit. The English version is slightly more prosaic and less certain in its origin. A kingpin can be either the axis about which steered wheels pivot in a motor vehicle (thus playing a very important role) or the headpin of the triangle of ten pins used in bowling. In colloquial use, kingpin is often heard in reference to mafia mobster leaders, though comic readers will also recognise him as a corpulent, cigar-smoking enemy of Spiderman. Someone best to keep onside in all circumstances…

To call the shots
Faire la pluie et le beau temps
(To make the rain and the fine weather)

The ball is in his court   La balle est dans son camp

It is better to talk to the organ-grinder than to his monkey
Mieux vaut s'adresser à Dieu qu'à ses saints
(Better to talk to God than his saints)

On the way out?
BIENTÔT CHEZ PÔLE EMPLOI

To have teething troubles
Essuyer les plâtres

This expression, meaning to have start-up or initial problems, dates from the 19th century in the French version. As any housebuilder or DIY buff knows, when the plasterwork ('les plâtres') is still wet on a new build, you don't want to be rubbing against it ('essuyer' – also to wipe/dry) with your best clothes on, since you will have a problem with both the walls and your dirty clothes. The English refers to the evident pain (and associated howls and tears) encountered when babies start to teethe for the first time. Best endured and overcome as quickly as possible – like the early stages of a new project.

To have your head in the clouds
Marcher à côté de ses pompes

A person of whom this is said would be an unwelcome co-worker. The English version suggests a day-dreamer who, rather than tackle practical problems, prefers to sit spaced out at their desk. The date and origin of the phrase are unknown. The French version, 'to walk to the side of one's pumps/shoes', dates from the 20th century, although the word 'pompes' is found in the 19th. Presumably the sense is that the person is so clueless he doesn't realise he hasn't got his shoes on, even though they are right beside him.

To be taken for a ride
Etre pris pour un pigeon

Not necessarily something one might want to do on a quiet Sunday afternoon, as it means to be duped, legged over or at best misled. The English version is even more sinister, since it has origins in the American underworld.

In the infamous gangster interfighting of the 1920s and '30s in many American cities, a perceived rival might be disposed of by being offered a ride into the woods on the pretext of a quiet chat from which they would almost certainly not return alive. In this context, to be taken for a pigeon, as the French are, would seem preferable. The expression dates from the 15th century, since when a 'pigeon' has been synonymous with an idiot or a dupe.

A schoolboy error   Une erreur de novice   *(A novice error)*

To twiddle your thumbs   Se tourner les pouces

A bad workman always blames his tools
Un méchant ouvrier ne saurait trouver de bon outil
(A bad worker would never know where to find a good tool)

A one-trick pony   Il n'a qu'un tour dans son sac
(He only has one turn in his bag)

To be in the firing line
Etre dans l'œil du tigre   *(To be in the eye of the tiger)*

To carry the can
Payer les pots cassés

...is to take responsibility or accountability for an action, even if it wasn't your own. The French version is first found at the start of the 17th century and implies a financial disadvantage to whoever is forced to take responsibility, since they are made to pay for the broken pots. The moral here is not to be left standing in close proximity to any shattered objects in a china shop. The origin of the 'can' in the English version, which dates from the 1930s, is uncertain. It may be military, referring to someone forced to replenish beer supplies and thus carry the can(s), or to coal mining, where the explosives are carried in a can. Finally it could refer to a poor unfortunate whose unhappy task is to empty the contents of a primitive loo and thus carry the can to dispose of the human sewage elsewhere. Paying for shards of porcelain seems a better option here.

To be the scapegoat
Etre la tête de Turc *(To be the Turk's head)*

The client bailed on me
Le client m'a fait faux bond *(The client made a fake leap)*

There's bad blood between the boss and him
Le torchon brûle entre le chef et lui
(The tea-towel burns between the boss and him)

To cock something up
Chier dans la colle (!) *(To crap in the glue)*

To take a sickie
Prendre un arrêt maladie bidon *(To take a phoney sick break)*

Up the creek without a paddle
Dans la mouise

A difficult situation from which you have no means of escape. The English version can also be found as the more vulgar 'to be up shit creek', which serves to reinforce the sense of desperation, since you really wouldn't want to try to swim for shore in such waters. This form has been known since the 1920s. The presence of excrement is also implied in the French version, which dates from the late 19th century. The word 'mouise' was commonly used then, as it is now, to mean poverty. However, in the early 1800s it could also mean a soup of really poor quality or (if you're squeamish look away here) faeces of diarrhoea consistency – something you definitely don't want to find yourself in!

To bite the dust   Mordre la poussière

The die is cast
Les carottes sont cuites
(The carrots are cooked)

The straw that broke the camel's back
La goutte d'eau qui a fait déborder le vase
(The drop of water which makes the vase overflow)

To go bust
Mettre la clé sous la porte   *(To put the key under the door)*

That's the last straw!
C'est la fin des haricots !
....

This expression, which means that something has become unbearable or untenable, often as a result of an apparently small action, is significantly older in English than French. The full version for Anglophones can be found as far back as the mid-17th century, but the most cited reference comes from Charles Dickens' *Dombey and Son* (1847–8), where the full phrase reads: 'As the last straw breaks the laden camel's back…' Without the same literary heritage, the French expression derives from two possible 'real-life' situations. The first refers to the fact that parlour games played at the start of the 20th century used beans as counters or tokens and thus when you had lost all your 'haricots' it was the end of the game. The second is more prosaic and suggests that in the same period beans were a staple part of the cheap diet provided in colleges, boarding schools, hospitals, prisons and similar institutions. If there were no more beans, there was literally nothing to eat and thus it could soon be 'The End' or 'Fin'.

To be on the dole
Travailler pour le premier employeur de France

An unhappy situation to be in, since this means to be out of work or unemployed. The use of 'dole' has been known (in British English at least) since the end of the First World War. To dole out something is to hand or give it out, and the expression refers to the unemployment benefit money you receive from the State when you are without another source of income. The French version is ironic, as there are more unemployed in France than there are civil servants, so the State does indeed hand out money, if not work, to more people than anyone else in the country. A wonderful euphemism.

To be suspended   Etre mis à pied   *(To be put on foot)*

To give someone the red card
Mettre un carton rouge à quelqu'un

To get the sack
Se faire limoger *(To be 'Limoged'; from the town of Limoges where a number of incapable generals were appointed to command by Maréchal Joffre during the First World War)*

To show someone the door
Se faire lourder   *('Lourde' is old French for door)*

Don't forget to check the answers to the quiz.
See how many you got right...

1. Se sortir les tripes
2. Etre au taquet au travail
3. Reçevoir cinq sur cinq
4. Avoir du pain sur la planche
5. Tirer les marrons du feu
6. Les carottes sont cuites
7. Tenir quelqu'un au jus

a) To slog your guts out
b) To be snowed under at work
c) To hear it loud and clear
d) To have a lot on your plate
e) To reap the benefits
f) The die is cast
g) To keep someone up to speed

PLAYTIME
APRÈS LE TURBIN

GOING OUT, STAYING IN, DINNER PARTY CONVERSATIONS, PLAYING WITH THE LOCALS AT PÉTANQUE…whatever you choose to do when not at work, this chapter should give you some expressions you might be lacking. Don't play too hard, or you might be heading for 'Game Over' sooner than expected!

Socialising or not...
CONVIVIAL OU PAS ...

To have forty winks
Coincer la bulle
....

...is to have a quick sleep, a cat-nap, a bit of shut-eye. The French expression has military origins and comes via the word for spirit level, 'niveau à bulle', which is used to ensure that an object is completely flat or level. In a military context the spirit level was used to check that the artillery guns were set up correctly, that those parts that needed to be level were not squint or at an angle. When the little air bubble ('bulle') on the measuring instrument was caught ('coincée') in between the two black lines, the gun was completely level. Their work done, the soldiers would have nothing else to do and thoughts might indeed shift to having a quick nap before battle commenced. The French expression thus can mean 'to have nothing to do', but more commonly means to do nothing horizontally, to have a quick siesta. The English version has been known since the late 1820s, with 'wink' referring to the short closing of the eye, though this is usually done while awake. Why we should take 40 of them in order to sleep is unknown, but it is generally accepted that this is a shut-eye which is not done in bed and usually best not done in meetings, presentations or other important ceremonies.

To be a wallflower Faire tapisserie (*To do tapestry*)

A bit pipe and slippers Pantouflard (*A slipper wearer*)

To be old school Etre vieux jeu (*To be old game*)

A couch potato Un cul-de-plomb (*A lead arse*)

An armchair athlete
Un sportif en chaise longue (*A deckchair sportsman*)

To thumb a book
Lire un livre en diagonale (*To read a book on the diagonal*)

To have a house-warming party
Pendre la crémaillère

Moving into a new residence always requires some form of celebration and the English express this by means of a 'house-warming'. This is easy to understand since a cold house is an unwelcome one and so, in the days before central heating, friends and family would bring firewood as a welcome gift and build fires in the entire house to warm it up. It was also believed that this would help ward off evil spirits, who would loiter in cold, empty places. The French variation dates from the 16th century, when all cooking was done on the hearth using a huge metal pot. This was hung from a chimney hook whose height could be adjusted depending on who was cooking. Building a new house creates an appetite and so one of the first things to be done in a completed French residence was to hang the chimney hook ('pendre la crémaillère') so that the lady of the house could whip up some well-deserved food for all the family, friends and neighbours who had helped build the new home. The expression has survived, even if cooking on the hearth has long since disappeared.

To go window shopping
Faire du lèche-vitrine

Not to be confused with acquiring some new double glazing, this means to do a tour of the shops without actually buying anything. The English version is obvious: you look in the shop windows and fantasise about what you could have. You probably won't enter the shop and even if you do you won't spend any money. The French version dates from the early 20th century and literally means to 'do window licking'. This sounds a particularly unpleasant pastime, not least for the unfortunate shopkeeper who would need to clean his or her windows thereafter. Since the 12th century, 'lécher' has meant to lick or run your tongue over something, but by the 19th century had taken on an additional meaning of to touch lightly or brush against something. This is the sense of the current expression – not that you actually lick the window, but that you get very close to it (perhaps within a tongue's length) in order to best view the tantalising objects on display.

To go on a pub crawl
Faire la tournée des grands ducs

Belying the myth that only the British indulge in drinking sessions, this expression means a long night of frequenting different bars or pubs. The end result, for the Anglophone, is that you are possibly so drunk that you can no longer walk upright but merely crawl between the drinking establishments. The French expression has a historical basis though the 'grands ducs' referred to were in fact Russian rather than French. At the end of the 19th century, members of the imperial family were frequent visitors to the newly remodelled Paris. In particular the Russian princes found much to amuse themselves and, with no need to work but in possession of lots of money, were often to be found staggering from cabaret to cabaret, bar to bar, in short from any source of pleasure to another until the wee hours of the morning. Some things don't change.

To be a night owl   Etre un oiseau de nuit

To dance as if you have two left feet
Danser comme un pied   (*To dance like a foot*)

To be tone-deaf
Ne pas avoir d'oreille   (*To have no ear*)

To paint the town red
Faire la bombe

...is to celebrate in style, live it up, party hard, have a blast. At first glance 'faire la bombe', to make the bomb, might seem to follow on from this last explosive meaning. In fact, the French expression derives from 'faire bombance', where 'bombance' means a feast, an auspicious grand occasion of eating and drinking, generally a time to let your hair down. 'Bombance' derives from the Old French 'bobance', which was known as far back as the 12th century, suggesting that the French have been partying for quite some time. The English version dates from the second half of the 19th century, and possibly comes from America. However, why it exists in this form is a matter of speculation: one theory suggests it is associated with red-light districts and might signal the end of a wild night out. Another propounds that it was hell-raising cowboys who threatened to paint a town red, if they weren't allowed to behave as they pleased. Alternatively, it could refer to the spilling of blood as revelries turned into fisticuffs, with a bloody nose to add to the throbbing headache the morning after.

Dressed up to the nines
Tiré à quatre épingles

....

To have your glad rags on
Etre sur son trente et un

....

To be wearing your very best clothes. Various theories have been put forward to explain the 'nines' in the English expression: that it is a corruption of the Old English 'to then eyne' or eyes, that it takes nine yards of material to make a good suit, that the men of the 99th Regiment of Foot were always well turned out, or to the pure quality of precious metals. In short, we don't know. The French versions are similarly unclear. The first, 'pulled by four pins', dates back to the early 19th century and probably refers to the number of pins required to hold a piece of material in place while making a dress or garment. The second version is more obscure. Some sources claim this refers to a 'trentain', a luxurious material made of 3,000 threads; others that it is the requisite number of points required to win a card game; or that it simply refers to the end-of-the-month payday, when people might be tempted to dress up and go out. However, the expression exists also as to be 'sur son trente-deux', 'trente-six', 'quarante-deux' and even 'cinquante-et-un'. Pick a number and dress accordingly!

She can't sing for toffee
Elle chante comme une casserole

....

Not great for those who enjoy a good tune, this expression, which means to sing very badly, is of uncertain origin in its English form. Possibly it is an ironic take on the old idea that travelling minstrels would sing for their supper, but that a bad performance wouldn't earn a paltry sweet, let alone a meal. Apart from a sticky bonbon, toffee also can mean rubbish or nonsense and so it is perhaps in this context that the toffee is applied. The French expression is equally ambiguous in origin. To understand why someone might sing like a saucepan ('casserole'), you first have to realise that they could also sing like a syringe ('seringue')! The latter dates from the early 19th century and is probably an amusing corruption of 'chanter comme une sirène', a reference to those mythical sirens/mermaids who sang to lure sailors to their doom. Why the shift from syringe to saucepan is anyone's guess, but one suggestion relates to the terrible din made by various metal pots and pans traditionally attached to the car of a just-married couple.

Fine feathers make fine birds
Les belles plumes font les beaux oiseaux

She smells like a tart's boudoir! Elle cocotte !
('Cocotter' is to have a strong smell; 'cocotte' is a loose woman)

Never discuss politics or religion
POLITIQUEMENT CORRECT

Trust-fund tree-huggers
Les écolos-bobos

We are not sure this exact expression exists in English, though we have met many who fit the description: well-meaning and well-to-do (middle-class) people with Green political leanings. Tree-hugger is a slightly pejorative and less militant term for an eco-warrior; a trust-fund (baby) is someone who is wealthy because of their family, rather than because of any money they have earned. Often they have no serious full-time employment, nor any need to earn a living, so tend to participate in a range of activities from shopping to drug abuse to political causes. The marriage of the two English characteristics takes us close to the recognised French expression. 'Ecolos' is short for 'les écologistes' and 'Bobos' are 'Bourgeois-Bohème'. Such people also answer to the description of 'gauche caviar' or champagne socialists. They are a plentiful source of satire for advocating a theoretical life by one set of values, while living by completely different and much more luxurious standards, most notably in the smartest arrondissements of Paris. Before you throw this book down in exasperation, we accept that these are all caricatural representations, and not everyone will agree with them. As such, this is a perfect example of why neither politics nor religion should be discussed in polite society or at the dinner table.

The little people (of France)
La France d'en bas

We felt this expression needed some background detail. The English version does not refer to children or those of diminished stature. Instead it is a (mildly) pejorative reference to the common man, the man on the street, those who make up the backbone of the country, but who are perceived to live 'normal', unremarkable lives. When used by politicians, it has a slightly paternalistic feel to it, as if only they (the big people) know what is best for the rest of us. The French expression also has this pejorative undertone. The phrase was famously used by a former French Prime Minister to divide France into two parts, 'd'en bas' and 'd'en haut'. These are respectively the lower, and implied inferior, and upper, and implied superior/elite echelons. It doesn't take a rocket scientist to work out that this might be polemical. We are going to stay well clear of any political hot potato and move onto religion instead...

Champagne socialist
Gauche caviar (*caviar left*)

To change your opinion as often as you change your socks
Changer d'avis comme de chemise
(*To change opinion like your shirt*)

To flip-flop
Retourner sa veste (*To turn your jacket inside-out*)

To change your tune
Changer son fusil d'épaule
(*To change your rifle to the other shoulder*)

To bury your head in the sand
La politique de l'autruche (*The ostrich politics*)

To have a skeleton in the closet
Avoir un cadavre dans le placard
(*To have a corpse in the cupboard*)

A spin doctor Un faiseur d'image (*A maker of images*)

Political double-talk
La langue de bois de la politique (*The wooden tongue of politics*)

To soft-soap someone
Passer la brosse à reluire à quelqu'un
(*To pass the shining brush to someone*)

A political big-wig
Un gros bonnet de la politique (*A big hat in politics*)

The man on the street Monsieur tout-le-monde (*Mr everyone*)

A happy clapper Une grenouille de bénitier (*A frog of the font*)

More Catholic than the Pope
Plus royaliste que le Roi (*More royalist than the king*)

And action!
ON TOURNE !

To run like the wind
Courir comme un dérané

...is to run very quickly, to run like mad or like a bat out of hell. The English version probably refers to the fact that the wind can 'move' at very high speeds, or that the faster you run, the more you feel the wind on your face. One source suggests the expression derives from the racing track, and those on horseback are often said to 'ride like the wind', but this may just be a nice theory. The French expression, on the other hand, dates back to the Ancient Greek practice of drying out the spleen ('la rate') of runners in order to improve their performance. Over time this became a surgical practice and, apparently as recently as the 18th century, unhappy dogs had their spleen removed ('dérater') in order to make them more animated or energetic, though with no empirical evidence that this worked. There were some who believed performing the same organ removal on a human might have a similar effect and so enable men to run at faster speeds. The current expression was first recorded in 1750, at which point such performance-enhancing surgery might have been conceivable. For the sake of French sprinters, one hopes the practice has now died out...

To set off hell for leather
Partir sur les chapeaux de roues

To depart very quickly, or at breakneck speed. The English version was first recorded in an 1888 work by Rudyard Kipling, *The Story of the Gadsbys*, and apparently originates with the British army in India. It may well be a reference to the weight of a man beating against the saddle as he galloped, or the leather boots kicking the horse into action. The current meaning can be applied to anything that moves at a very high speed. The French version has nothing to do with hats, 'chapeaux', as most understand the word. 'Les chapeaux de roues' in this context are actually the hubcaps on the wheels, and the sense is that of a car cornering at great speed. The vehicle inclines such that it almost seems that the wheels, and thus the hubcaps, on the inside of the bend touch the ground. Since hubcaps are a 20th-century invention, we can date the expression to some time during this period.

Step on it!
Appuie sur le champignon !

This expression, which means to hit the gas or accelerate, is more or less self-explanatory in the English version. The 'it' refers to the accelerator/gas pedal and the 'step' to placing your foot on it. Easy. The literal translation of the French, 'press on the mushroom', is slightly more bewildering until we go back to the start of the 20th century and remember how different cars were back then. The accelerator in particular was not so much a flat metal pedal as it is nowadays, but rather a long stalk with a metal semicircle on top which looked very much like a mushroom in shape. Hence when you wanted to accelerate in France in those days you stepped on the metal mushroom!

To get cracking Enclencher la première *(To put it into first gear)*

To go at full pelt
Aller à fond de train *(To go at the maximum pace)*

A Sunday driver Un conducteur du dimanche

Whiplash Le coup du lapin *(The rabbit blow)*

To drive at breakneck speed
Rouler à tombeau ouvert *(To drive with an open tomb)*

To ski like Bambi on ice
Skier comme une luge à foin *(To ski like a hay sledge)*

To swim like a brick Nager comme une brique

A landlubber Un marin d'eau douce *(A freshwater sailor)*

To get back to dry land
Arriver sur le plancher des vaches *(To get to the cows' floor)*

To get a second wind Avoir un second souffle

To be neck and neck Etre coude à coude *(To be elbow to elbow)*

By the skin of your teeth A un poil près *(By just a hair)*

To get your skates on
Avoir intérêt à faire vinaigre

In other words to get a move on, hurry up; often used as an order. Skates have existed in the English language since the 17th century, possibly from the old Northern French 'eschace', and were originally of the ice variety, but are now also found in roller versions. Whichever you choose, and slightly depending on your level of ability, you should go faster on skates than on foot. Hence, to get your skates on is to do something at a greater speed. The French version has a charming history which belies the acidic nature of vinegar itself. Its roots are in a children's skipping game and date back to the start of the 19th century. Possibly basing their choice on condiments that were seen on the table – oil and vinegar – the children adopted the more unctuous, slower moving liquid to denote a slower speed at which a skipping rope turned, and thus vinegar for the faster speed. By shouting out 'huille' or 'vinaigre' as you jumped over the rope, you could ask your playmates to change the tempo. Whether they did as you asked was another matter.

To hit the bull's eye
Faire mouche

This expression, which can be used literally as well as idiomatically in both languages, means that you have hit the centre of the target, or nailed something. The earliest record of the English version dates from the 1830s and is used in reference to military shooting/rifle targets. 'Bull's eye' had existed in a 'sporting' metaphoric sense long before this, being a means of gambling in the violent sport of bull-baiting. It first referred to putting a bet on whether the dogs or the bull would win, and then came to mean a coin. At an unknown later date it came to stand for the target itself, presumably due to the similarity of this bovine eye and a shooting target. The French also refer to an animal, a fly, and have done so since the end of the 19th century. This is due to the colour and shape of the insect, which looks broadly like the black centre circle of the target, and possibly seems just as large to someone aiming from a great distance.

Game over!
FIN DE PARTIE !

To spend the night in the nick
Passer la nuit au violon

This expression implies someone has behaved very badly, even criminally, since it means that they slept in a prison cell. 'Nick' is British slang for jail and means the same as 'slammer' or 'pen' in North America. But why? 'Nick' is actually a very old English word which can mean to make a notch, but also since the early 17th century has meant to be arrested or be in prison. Interestingly, the use of 'nick' as a verb meaning to steal originated only in the 19th century. The French version is slightly less obvious, since to spend a night in a violin seems a spatial impossibility. In fact, 'violon' has meant prison in French since the late 1790s and possibly derives from the similarity between the strings on the instrument and the bars on the cell, but the exact origin is unknown.

To back the wrong horse   Miser sur le mauvais cheval

To win hands down   Arriver dans un fauteuil
(To arrive in an armchair)

To beat someone hollow
Battre quelqu'un à plates coutures   *(To beat someone to flat seams)*

To throw in the towel
Jeter l'éponge

Both of these expressions, meaning to give up or in, derive from the boxing ring, or more accurately prize-fighting. This early type of pugilism, often bare-knuckle fights, typically had few rules and so, when one boxer was deemed to have no fight left in him, his coach would signal to the referee or opposing team that his man was beaten. This he did by means of throwing the towel, which was used to wipe blood and sweat away in between rounds, into the ring. In some quarters, a sponge was used instead and this is the origin of the French expression, which also exists in identical English and Italian versions. There is another idiom in French which means to give up, often used in guessing games or when one hasn't a clue about something: 'donner sa langue au chat', to give your tongue to the cat.

To be six feet under
Etre entre quatre planches

If you are this in either language then you are not in a good way...in fact you are dead. Technically speaking you are dead and buried. The English expression probably dates back to the Great Plague of 1665 when the authorities issued edicts to ensure that all corpses of plague victims were buried sufficiently deep, i.e. no less than 6 feet (1.8 metres) underground, in order to minimise the risk of contagion. Daniel Defoe's fictional account of the plague (over 50 years later), which reports on such burial edicts, may have helped disseminate the use of the expression in common parlance. The French equivalent is confusing for those who assume that a coffin should be made of six planks of wood in order to be robust, since the literal translation is 'to be between four planks'. However, if you exclude the lid and the base of the coffin from the count, even the most pedantic should be satisfied. When the phrase came to existence is unknown, but since one of the chapters of Victor Hugo's epic *Les Misérables* (1882) is called 'Entre quatre planches' we can date it to the mid-19th century at least.

To send someone to their maker
Faire avaler son acte de naissance à quelqu'un
(To make someone swallow their birth certificate)

To be pushing up daisies   Manger les pissenlits par la racine
(To eat the dandelions by their roots)

To croak   Casser sa pipe   *(To break your pipe)*

To kick the bucket
Passer l'arme à gauche

This expression, yet another one meaning to die, is difficult to pin down in both the French and English versions. Kicking the bucket could refer to a method of committing suicide by hanging, where kicking away the bucket you are standing on causes the 'coup de grâce'. It could also refer to a method of slaughtering pigs whereby the bucket (derived from the French 'buquet') is a receptacle held under the animal to catch the blood as it drains out. This would inevitably be kicked by a trotter in the death throes. A (less ghastly) version reflects the custom in pre-Reformation days of a bucket being filled with holy water and placed by the feet of a laid-out corpse for well-wishers to sprinkle on the deceased as a mark of respect. The French version, to move your weapon to the left side, equally has a number of possible origins. One derives from fencing, where forcing an adversary to move his foil from right to left hand would leave him almost defenceless and thus easy to kill. Another dates back to Napoleonic times when, in order to reload, soldiers were forced to place their weapons on the ground on their left-hand side, thus leaving them vulnerable to enemy fire. The most likely is that for French soldiers 'repos' or 'at ease' requires them to place their rifle on their left foot. It is a small step from 'repos' to 'le repos eternal' or eternal sleep…. Good night. Bonne nuit.

QUIZ ANSWERS

Don't forget to check the answers to the quiz.
See how many you got right…

1. A couch potato	a) Un cul-de-plomb
2. To win hands down	b) Arriver dans un fauteuil
3. To be pushing up daisies	c) Manger les pissenlits par la racine
4. To get back to dry land	d) Arriver sur le plancher des vaches
5. A happy clapper	e) Une grenouille de bénitier
6. To go at full pelt	f) Aller à fond de train

Glossary/Glossaire

aboyer	to bark
anguille (f)	eel
as (m)	ace (cards)
astiquer	to polish
aveugle	blind
bague (f)	ring
balai (m)	broom
barreau (m)	rung/bar (of cage)
baskets (fpl)	trainers/sneakers
bénitier (m)	font (in church)
bique (f)	nanny goat
borgne (m)	one-eyed man
bosse (f)	bump
bouc (m)	billy goat
bouchée (f)	mouthful
bourreau (m)	executioner/hangman
bourrer	to cram/fill up
bourrique (f)	ass/donkey
braise (f)	embers
brebis galeuse (f)	a sheep with scabies
bride (f)	bridle
brouiller	to blur
charretier (m)	carter/porter
châtier	to punish
chier	to shit
cintrer	to bend/curve
clopinette (f)	cigarette butt
clou (m)	nail
coing (m)	quince
colleuse (f)	sticker/licker
collier (m)	collar (of animal), necklace
coude (m)	elbow
couleuvre (f)	grass snake
cracher	to spit
crapaud (m)	toad
crapuleux/se	villainous
cuisse (f)	thigh (of human), leg (of chicken or frog)
déborder	to overflow
déboutonner	to unbutton
eau douce (f)	freshwater
échelle (f)	ladder
épinard (m)	spinach
fauteuil (m)	armchair
fendre	to split
fil (m)	wire
forçat (m)	convict
forgeron (m)	blacksmith
fouine (f)	stone marten, an animal of the weasel family
froc (m)	trousers
frotter	to rub
fusil (m)	rifle
gale (f)	scabies/mange
galon (m)	braid/stripe (military)
gaspiller	to waste
gerbe (f)	spray (usually of flowers)
glaçon (m)	ice cube
gond (m)	hinge
guenon (f)	female monkey
gueule (f)	mouth (of an animal, or in slang of a human)
jaquette (f)	morning coat, also a cardigan
jaillir	to flood/gush out
jupon (m)	petticoat
levrette (f)	greyhound bitch
limande (f)	dab/sole (fish)
luge (f)	sledge
malin	smart/shrewd
marmite (f)	cooking pot
martel or marteau (m)	hammer (old)
merlan (m)	whiting
moine (m)	monk
mouler	to mould/shape
os (m)	bone
oursin (m)	sea urchin
outre (f)	goatskin
pactole (m)	goldmine
paille (f)	straw
passoire (f)	sieve
peigne (m)	comb
pelle (f)	shovel
pendre	to hang
péter	to fart
pétrin (m)	kneading machine
pierre (m)	stone/pebble
piquer	to sting/bite (by insect)
plancher (m)	floor
poil (m)	hair
puce (f)	flea
rayer	to scratch
rombière (f)	old biddy, old bag
scier	to saw
se méfier	to be wary
se mouiller	to get wet
secouer	to shake
sucer	to suck
tailler	to cut/sharpen
tambour (m)	drum
tapisserie (f)	tapestry
taquet (m)	wedge
taupe (m)	mole (animal)
tronche (f)	'mug' i.e. face
troupeau (m)	flock
volée (f)	flight
volet (m)	shutter

Index

To be a night owl 189
To be a right nosy parker 12
To be a scaredy cat 14
To be a smash hit 174
To be a wallflower 187
To be a workshy soap dodger 24
To be able to hold your drink 148
To be about to lose your cookies 78
To be all fingers and thumbs 14
To be all mouth and no trousers 12
To be all sweetness and light 29
To be an old hand 71
To be an old soak 148
To be as bald as a coot 65
To be as busy as a bee 170
To be as high as a kite 20
To be as right as rain 73
To be at death's door 75
To be Bank Holiday weather 95
To be blowing a hooley 97
To be bone idle 20
To be bored stiff 86
To be born with a silver spoon in your mouth 163
To be caught between a rock and a hard place 139
To be caught red-handed 128
To be cross-eyed 72
To be done in two shakes of a lamb's tail 115
To be fed up to the back teeth 89
To be filthy rich 166
To be full of beans 109
To be full to bursting 147
To be getting on a bit 71
To be going places 175
To be half cut 150
To be hand in glove 41
To be head and shoulders above the rest 175
To be hoist by your own petard 124
To be horny 55
To be in the boss's good books 175
To be in the firing line 180
To be in the red 154
To be in your birthday suit 59
To be just skin and bones 66
To be left high and dry 127
To be like a caged lion 132
To be like two peas in a pod 79
To be mad as a box of frogs 21
To be neck and neck 196
To be no spring chicken! 71
To be old school 187
To be on tenterhooks 131
To be on the dole 183
To be out of your tree 19
To be over the moon 84
To be packed like sardines 169
To be pissed off 89
To be pissing it down 95
To be power hungry 177
To be pushing up daisies 198
To be rolling in it 165
To be sharp-set 146
To be six feet under 199
To be snowed under at work 170
To be soaked to the skin 95

To be stood up 47
To be suspended 183
To be taken for a ride 179
To be the apple of someone's eye 43
To be the boss's blue-eyed boy 176
To be the scapegoat 181
To be tone-deaf 189
To be up to your eyeballs in debt 154
To be worth your weight in gold 173
To beat someone hollow 198
To bite the dust 182
To black out 75
To blow one's own trumpet 42
To blow your top 132
To bounce a cheque 162
To bow and scrape 176
To bring grist to the mill 169
To bring home the bacon 166
To build castles in the air 140
To burn the candle at both ends 138
To bury your head in the sand 193
To buy a pig in a poke 162
To call a spade a spade 110
To call the shots 178
To carry coals to Newcastle 130
To carry the can 180
To champ at the bit 132
To change your opinions as often as you change your socks 193
To change your tune 193
To choke the chicken 58
To cock something up 181
To come clean 109
To cost an arm and a leg 155
To cough up 159
To cover your tracks 121
To croak 198
To cry wolf 39
To cry your heart out 48
To dance as if you had two left feet 189
To dip your wick 59
To do a moonlight flit 161
To do a technicolour yawn 78
To do something off the cuff 113
To down in one 148
To drink like a fish 148
To drive at breakneck speed 196
To drive someone round the bend 89
To drown your sorrows 150
To earn your bread and butter 163
To earn your spurs 174
To eat humble pie 112
To eat like a bird 146
To eat like a pig 146
To fall in love at the drop of a hat 47
To feel like death warmed up 75
To feel under the weather 75
To feel your hackles rising 132
To find the perfect match 46
To find your soulmate 44
To flick the bean 58
To flip-flop 193
To fly off the handle 133
To fob someone off 162
To follow orders to the letter 111
To fudge the issue 122

To get a dressing-down 38
To get a second wind 196
To get an eyeful 55
To get back into the harness 169
To get back to dry land 196
To get cracking 195
To get down to business 169
To get lucky 58
To get on like a house on fire 40
To get the sack 183
To get your skates on 196
To give a blow job 59
To give a leg up to someone 176
To give someone a lot of rope 42
To give someone the red card 183
To give someone the rough side of your
tongue 34
To go and see a man about a dog 77
To go at full pelt 195
To go bust 182
To go commando 69
To go Dutch 160
To go like a barn door in the wind 56
To go like a train 56
To go off at a tangent 14
To go on a pub crawl 188
To go through money like water 159
To go window shopping 188
To goose someone 56
To grab a quick bite 145
To grease someone's palm 166
To have a bat in the cave 73
To have a body like a badly packed
kitbag 65
To have a bun in the oven 61
To have a cushy job 174
To have a face for radio 65
To have a face like a bag of spanners 65
To have a face like a bulldog chewing a
wasp 65
To have a frog in your throat 73
To have a good head for business 173
To have a hard knock life 154
To have a house-warming party 187
To have a lot on your plate 170
To have a memory like an elephant 80
To have a mind like a sewer 56
To have a poker up your arse 14
To have a raging temperature 73
To have a screw loose 23
To have a sharp tongue 38
To have a short fuse 133
To have a six-pack 67
To have a skeleton in the closet 193
To have a stonking hangover 150
To have a turtlehead 78
To have an ace up your sleeve 115
To have bags under your eyes 73
To have bats in the belfry 22
To have been around the block a few times 71
To have been dropped on your head as a child 23
To have blinkers on 17
To have butterflies in your stomach 72
To have fallen from the ugly tree and
hit every branch on the way down 64
To have forty winks 186

To have had one too many 150
To have it up to here 89
To have itchy feet 132
To have lost your marbles 21
To have mended your ways 29
To have more than one string to your bow 111
To have other fish to fry 110
To have teething troubles 179
To have the luck of the Irish 30
To have the Midas touch 166
To have the munchies 146
To have the shakes 71
To have the trots 78
To have the wool pulled over your eyes 17
To have wandering hands 56
To have your glad rags on 191
To have your head in the clouds 179
To have your nose close to the
grindstone 170
To hear it loud and clear 177
To hide the sausage 59
To hit a snag 128
To hit the bull's eye 197
To hit the jackpot 166
To hit the nail on the head 111
To hold all the trumps 29
To keep someone up to speed 177
To keep your ear to the ground 111
To kick the bucket 199
To kick yourself 125
To kill two birds with one stone 113
To know something like the back of your
hand 174
To know the score 29
To know your onions 172
To laugh one's head off 115
To laugh up your sleeve 122
To let the cat out of the bag 18
To lick your chops 146
To lie through your teeth 120
To line your pockets 162
To live a hand-to-mouth existence 153
To live life to the full 29
To live like a lord 166
To look like the back end of a bus 65
To make a mint 166
To make a mountain out of a molehill 135
To make believe that the moon is made of
green cheese 119
To make puppy dog's eyes at someone 44
To make sheep's eyes at someone 43
To meet someone half way 42
To miss the boat 141
To moonlight 170
To move heaven and earth 111
To never say a word 12
To nit-pick 141
To paddle your own canoe 29
To paint the town red 189
To park a tiger 78
To pay on the nail 163
To pay someone back in spades 51
To play gooseberry 44
To play hooky 19
To play pocket billiards 58
To poo your pants 78

Bibliography

Dictionnaire d'Expressions et Locutions, Alain Rey and Sophie Chantreau, Le Robert, 2007

A la Queue Leu Leu, Gilles Guilleron, Editions First-Gruend, 2008

La Puce à l'Oreille, Claude Duneton, Le Livre de Poche, 1990

La Fin des Haricots, Colette Guillermard, Editions Bartillat, 2009

Expressions Françaises, Pascale Perrier and Michel Boucher, Editions Oskarson, 2010

Les Animaux Expressions Françaises, Pascale Perrier and Michel Boucher, Editions Oskarson, 2010

Les 1001 Expressions Préférées des Français, Georges Planelles, Les Editions de l'Opportun

Les Expressions Idiomatiques, Marie-Dominique Porée-Rongier, Editions First-Gruend, 2009

Colloquial French, C.W.E. Kirk-Greene, Foulsham, 1992

Sky My Husband!, Ciel Mon Mari!, Jean-Loup Chiflet, Editions Points, 2008

Les Expressions qui ont fait L'histoire, Bernard Klein, Librio, 2008

You Can't Get Blood out of a Turnip, Ilia Terzulli Warner and Christopher Arnander, Stacey International, 2007

Red Herrings and White Elephants, Albert Jack, Metro Publishing, 2004

Shaggy Dogs and Black Sheep, Albert Jack, Penguin Books, 2005

Oxford Dictionary of Proverbs, Jennifer Speake (ed), Oxford University Press, 2008

Spilling the Beans on the Cat's Pyjamas, Judy Parkinson, Michael o'Mara Books Limited, 2009

A Word in your Shell-like, Nigel Rees, HarperCollins Publishers, 2004

Dictionary of English Idioms, Daphne M. Gulland and David Hinds-Howell, Penguin Books, 2002

Dictionary of Idioms and their Origins, Linda and Roger Flavell, Kyle Books, 2006

Acknowledgements

We would like to thank Alan and Janette, Richard and Ali, Di, Patrick, Sylvie and all others who helped us create this book. Special thanks also to Vicki, our editor, and all the team at Kyle Books for helping us turn our idea into a reality.